MARRIAGE CUSTOMS AND CEREMONIES IN WORLD RELIGIONS

ARUN S. ROY, Ph.D.

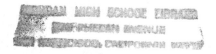

TRAFFORD

TRAFFORD PUBLISHING, VICTORIA, B.C. CANADA

Presented to _____

With Best Wishes

By _____

Date _____

Place _____

Note for Librarians: a cataloguing record for this book that includes Dewey Decimal
Classification and US Library of Congress numbers is available from the Library and Archives
of Canada. The complete cataloguing record can be obtained from their online database at:
www.collectionscanada.ca/amicus/index-e.html
ISBN 1-4120-3848-0
Printed in Victoria, BC, Canada

Cover Design : Shubhayan Roy

Word Processing and Editing : Amelie Valois

*Printed on paper with minimum 30% recycled fibre. Trafford's print shop runs on "green energy" from solar,
wind and other environmentally-friendly power sources.*

TRAFFORD

Offices in Canada, USA, Ireland and UK
This book was published *on-demand* in cooperation with Trafford Publishing. On-demand
publishing is a unique process and service of making a book available for retail sale to the
public taking advantage of on-demand manufacturing and Internet marketing. On-demand
publishing includes promotions, retail sales, manufacturing, order fulfilment, accounting and
collecting royalties on behalf of the author.

Book sales for North America and international:
Trafford Publishing, 6E–2333 Government St.,
Victoria, BC v8t 4p4 CANADA
phone 250 383 6864 (toll-free 1 888 232 4444)
fax 250 383 6804; email to orders@trafford.com
Book sales in Europe:
Trafford Publishing (uk) Ltd., Enterprise House, Wistaston Road Business Centre,
Wistaston Road, Crewe, Cheshire cw2 7rp UNITED KINGDOM
phone 01270 251 396 (local rate 0845 230 9601)
facsimile 01270 254 983; orders.uk@trafford.com
Order online at:
trafford.com/04-1656

10 9 8 7 6 5 4 3

TABLE OF CONTENTS

Chapter 4
Some Regional Variations in Hindu
Marriage Ceremony

   1.Oriya wedding 2. Tamil wedding 3.Telegu
   wedding 4. Gujrati wedding5. Punjabi wedding.
   6.Maharashtrian wedding. 7.Malayali wedding
   8.Kannada wedding. 9.Marwari wedding.
   10.Rajasthani wedding. 11.Sindhi wedding.
   12.Bengali wedding 13. Brahmo Samaj wedding
   14. Arya Samaj wedding 15. Assamese wedding
   16. Kashmiri wedding

Chapter 5
Muslim Marriage

Chapter 6
Sikh Marriage

Chapter 7
Buddhist Marriage

Chapter 8
Jain Marriage

Chapter 9
Zoroastrian (Parsi) Marriage

List of photographs (Appendix B)

1. A Japanese bride.
2. A bride from Punjab.
3. In a Punjabi wedding, bangles are given by the groom.
4. Sindur-Daan in a Bengali Hindu wedding ceremony.
5. A galaxy of Indian brides and bridegrooms in colorful and varied outfits.
6. A Konkani (South India) couple after their wedding ceremony.
7. A resident of Canada comes to the bride's house on horseback, recapturing the past tradition.
8. A traditional Buddhist wedding procession in the island of Bali.
9. A close relative offering 'Saki' to the bride in a Japanese wedding ceremony.
10. A Moroccan Muslim wedding.
11. Purification ceremony in a Japanese wedding.
12. Pala Ceremony in a Sikh Wedding.
13. A bride from the southern province of Andhra Pradesh, India.
14. A bride's left palm decorated with Mehendi or Henna colour.
15. An Indian couple newly married according to Jain wedding ceremony.
16. Mala-Badal (exchanging flower garlands) in a Bengali Hindu Ceremony.
17. A tribal bride from Ladakh near Kashmir, India.
18. A bride from U.P.—one of the northern provinces of India.
19. Khetubah, a decorative marriage contract in Jewish wedding.
20. 'Kanya-Daan' (also called 'Sampradaan') ceremony (bestowing the daughter by the father to the groom) in a Hindu wedding.
21. Sindoor-Daan ceremony (putting vermillion mark on forehead of the bride by the groom as a symbol of married status) in a Hindu wedding.
22. Shubha-Dristi (auspicious meeting of the eyes) in a Bengali Hindu wedding ceremony.

23. A newly married bride from the hilly region of Himachal Pradesh, India.
24. A Muslim Bengali Bride from Bangladesh
25. Laja-homa Ceremony (offering puffed rice to fire) in a Hindu Wedding .
26. The "Chuppah" Ceremony in a Jewish Wedding.
27. A Zoroastrian priest reciting blessings from the Zend Avesta in a Parsi wedding ceremony.
28. A couple taking seven steps or vows (Sapta-Padi) circling fire as the witness.
29. An Indoor Chuppa in a Jewish Wedding Ceremony.
30. Phool Sajja (Bed of Flowers) or 'Suhaag Raat' (Romantic Night) after the wedding.
31.A Christian Couple newly married in an exotic resort.
32. A newly wed Muslim Bride from Pakistan.
33. A Pakistani Muslim groom arriving for his wedding ceremony at the bride's house
34. An Indian sculpture showing a man offering a ring to her girlfriend
35. Newly married bride offering prayers at the sacred 'Tulsi' plant.
36. Kadholi ceremony---collecting water for ceremonial bath ('Mangal Snan') in a Punjabi wedding.
37. Exchanging flower garlands (Mala-Badal) in a Hindu ceremony.
38. Palki (palanquin) used in olden days to transport a bride.
39. Artistically decorated Palkis used by royal households.
40. Dolls- A Hindu Rajput couple of Rajasthan, India.
41. 'Sindur-Daan' Ceremony, putting red vermillion on the new bride as mark of the married status in a Hindu Wedding.
42. An Arya Samaj wedding ceremony.
43. An Indo-Canadian Bengali bride, after the wedding ceremony.
44. An Indonesian Muslim bride and a Bosnian Muslim groom.
45. A Japanese bride with her bridesmaid.
46. "Chautha" or the fourth day after wedding in a Muslim marriage.

47. An indoor 'Mandap' (canopy) commonly used for North Indian weddings.

48. An outdoor 'Mandap' (canopy) used for many North Indian weddings.

FOREWORD

One of the beautiful things about being Canadian is that without leaving home, we can experience the cultural diversity of the four corners of the globe. From a Christian church to a Hindu temple , from a Sikh gurdwara to a Muslim mosque to a Jewish synagogue, we live together.

One of the moments in my life that really highlighted the uniqueness of Canada, followed the firebombing of a Hindu temple in my hometown of Hamilton. To rebuild the temple, a fundraising committee included the whole community. Religious and non-religious groups, Hindus and non-Hindus came together in a celebration of the diversity that is our great country.

It was not always that way. When the first multiculuralism law in the world was introduced by Prime Minister Pierre Elliot Trudeau in the 1970's, there was criticism and opposition across the country. Over the years we have learned about each other and in learning about each other, we have learned to like each other and to live together as friends and family.

In learning about customs, rituals and religious underpinnings of each community, we will grow stronger together. Hopefully, contributions to the dialogue by writers like Dr. Arun Roy will help the world to grow stronger through knowledge. The road to peace is achieved through the pen, not the bomb. In his interesting and comprehensive book on marriage, Dr. Roy traces the evolution of marriage customs and ceremonies to religious traditions and geographic history. It is particularly interesting to note that several of the customs which are apparently very different in different religious practices and traditions often evolved from some common roots. His short discussion of the evolution of different religions, in the context of which marriage customs and ceremonies should be placed, would be found particularly useful by those not so familiar with the different religious faiths, philosophies, and customs.

Sheila Copps ,
Former Deputy Prime Minister of Canada and Minister of Canadian Heritage

To my wife, Jayanti,

For her constant encouragement and inspiration

Preface

In recent years I had the opportunity to attend quite a number of Hindu and interfaith wedding ceremonies in USA and Canada, mostly of the sons and daughters of our family friends. In these interfaith marriages often the bride was of the Hindu faith and the groom belonged to a different religious denomination or vice versa.

The Hindu wedding rituals and customs are fairly extensive and complex and are based upon age-old religious traditions. The new younger generation of potential brides and bridegrooms is curious and inquisitive. These young brides and grooms getting married according to Hindu faith and tradition often wonder how these ceremonies evolved and what the different customs signify. When I was approached personally, I was unable to refer them to a short but easily readable book for a broad understanding of these. This is what prompted me to start writing this book, originally on the religious and historical significance of the various customs and traditions in the Hindu marriages.

If writing the book on the Hindu marriage ceremonies was like a journey, I was advised by some readers to extend this journey a little further to explore the wedding customs and ceremonies that are followed in other world religions and faiths as well. The purpose of this book is to provide a quick glimpse of the wedding ceremonies and customs in Hinduism and other religions ---

Buddhism, Jainism, Islam, Christianity, Sikhism, Judaism and Zoroastrianism. The book deals with how the customs evolved over time and what these meant in the context of the religion and in the broad historical context. An attempt has also been made, wherever relevant, to indicate how the wedding rituals and customs that are practiced under different religious faiths are similar to or are different from one another. It became evident in the course of this journey that *although the customs and ceremonies were and still are very diverse across religious faiths and across geographic boundaries, there is an underlying thread of unity.*

Marriage customs and wedding ceremonies derive their meaning and significance from the religious faiths. For a proper understanding and appreciation of the marriage customs and ceremonies, it is essential to have a background of the respective religions. The author hopes that the prefatory remarks on the essence of each of the religious faiths and the Miscellaneous Notes (MN) placed at the end of the book will be found useful by those who are not so familiar with the living world religions and their background. They provide a useful context to situate the wedding rituals. Wherever relevant, original texts and scriptures have been consulted but in the interest of general readers presentation style has been kept simple and not burdened with elaborate and complex footnotes. However, Miscellaneous Notes (MN) at the end provide enough materials for more in-depth research into specific issues and aspects.

The chapter on wedding songs, the author hopes, will be found to be of particular interest to ethnologists and writers on multicultural themes. These wedding songs are truly a mirror of social customs associated with marriage and married life.

1719 Silver Bark Avenue   Arun S. Roy
Ottawa, K1C 7A9
CANADA
(Tel. : 613-837-1936)

ACKNOWLEDGEMENTS

The author is grateful to numerous individuals without whose willing cooperation and help, this book could not have been completed. Several individual priests and scholars provided comments and clarification on many aspects of the religious ceremony. Numerous other individuals were generous to give hours and hours of their valuable time for being interviewed on many regional details. Many others helped with the compilation of bridal songs which are becoming a vanishing tradition.

The author is particularly grateful to Pandit Ogoti P. Sarma, Pandit Dr. M. Shasrabuddhe and Pandit Murli of the Hindu Temple of Ottawa, Rabbi Dr. Reuven Bulka of Ottawa, Dr. John Samuel, Dr. Karnail Singh, Dr.Bhavani Nair, Kaveri Mahadevan, Vasanthi Gorur, Sheila Sharma, Syed Faruq, High Commission of Sri Lanka, Mohd. Jalaluddin, Malvinder Rakhra, and many others for their comments and suggestions. However, the author is responsible for any error or misinterpretation.

The author is also grateful to many others whose contribution in the form of photographs and texts considerably enriched this book :

Melanie and Shiro Shintaku, Soma Chatterjee, Ruma Tapadar, Piyali Basuroy, Tina Bose, David Todd, Vikas Kamat, Bobby Raj, Lynn Raha, Auditi Seal, Editor, *Perspectives India* , "Indian Brides : Symbol of Pristine Beauty", August 1998, Columbia

University Press, Jeanne Hanssen of MP Artworks, Retno and Senad Biber, Lind Luque (Imkluque), and Jatinder Pal Singh.

I am also grateful to Sheila Copps, former Deputy Prime Minister of Canada and Minister of Heritage Canada, for writing the Foreword for the book .

Arun S. Roy

Chapter 1

The Evolution of Marriage As An Institution

1.1 Introduction

Marriage is undoubtedly the most significant event in anybody's life—man or woman, rich or poor, big or small . It enriches family and social life in many ways and brings unique joy and happiness in one's life. But marriage also brings new responsibilities and duties and changes the process of interaction with other people.
Marriage can be defined as a union, a partnership between a man and a woman, known in society as husband and wife respectively and recognized as such under the law and under acceptable religious and social customs. That is, it is a union between members of the opposite sex and is usually formalized at a religious ceremony or according to a legal process . The roles and responsibilities of the husband and wife include living together, having sexual relations with one another, and are recognized as the parents of their offsprings.
 The process of evolution of marriage as an institution and as a formalized relation between man and woman is shrouded in mystery. In the primitive society, physical force of men folk was the basis of the relation between man and woman.

Instead of footnotes, some details are placed at the end of the book under the title " Miscellaneous Notes" (MN---numbered).

There is a broad consensus among social historians that sometime in the course of evolution of human civilisation a need was felt for regulating the relation between man and woman. This need was felt possibly for two reasons---economic and social.

First, as the concept of private property took its root, it became necessary to frame man-made laws to regulate the rights to property of the descendants.

Secondly, it became necessary to introduce the custom of marriage in the interest of imposing and preserving social order and harmony. Thus a socio-religious legal system came into being that broadly defined a relation between sexes that was socially acceptable and legally enforceable. This is the conclusion that historians have reached by piecing together the folklores, ancient religious epics and scriptures, and books of literature and chronicles that have survived the ravages of time.

1.2 Marriage and Private Property

In the early primitive society, men and women "followed animal instincts wholly without restraint so that no woman had her appointed husband". With the progress of civilisation, there was a transition from the promiscuity of lower mammals to the marriages of primitive men. Some historians like Will Durant (*Our Oriental Heritage : Story of Our Civilisation*) are of the opinion that initially some powerful economic motives favored the evolution of the institution of marriage and to formally regulate the relationship between man and woman. These motives were connected with the rising institution of private property, as mentioned above. Individual marriages came through the desire of the male to have cheap slaves, and to avoid bequeathing his property to other men's children.

For a detailed history of evolution of types of marriage, see Will Durant, *The Story of Our Civilization*, Vol.I.

1.3 Three Types of Marriage

Social historians who have done extensive research into the evolution of marriage as an institution find evidences of three types of marriage in human history. These are :

- Marriage by capture or force,
- Marriage by service, and
- Marriage by purchase.

Marriage By Capture

Among the primitive tribes, the women were always fought for by men, and the strongest man won. This is what sociologists today describe as *Marriage by capture or force*. In the primitive times of tribal warfare, women were considered to be an important form of wealth for the survival of a tribe or clan. The numerical superiority of a tribe determined its chances for survival. And for the numerical growth of population of a tribe , reproduction was essential. This explains why some fertility rituals are observed in wedding ceremonies even to this day in many parts of the world, even though we are not often conscious of the origin of such rituals and practices.

Marriage By Service

Marriage by capture in course of time gave rise to marriage by service. One of the most ancient examples of this kind of marriage is to be found in the Old Testament in the story of Jacob and Laban. According to this custom, the husband toils for the wife's father for a certain period of time until she is won as the reward for his services. Justification for this kind of marriage was that the husband compensates the bride's family for the expense incurred and care given to the girl in bringing her up to adulthood. This form of marriage still prevails among some tribes in the Middle East, South Asian countries, and among Red Indians in North America. Marriage by service gradually disappeared from the modern civilised community.

Marriage by Purchase

As wealth grew, it became more convenient to offer the father of the bride a substantial sum of money or goods for his daughter, rather than serve for her in an alien clan. Consequently marriage by purchase and parental arrangement became the rule in the more civilised societies. It was a natural development of patriarchal institutions ; father owns the daughter, and may dispose of her, as he sees fit. The concept that the father owns the daughter still prevails in the modern society to this day. This is evidenced by the practice observed in one form or another in most religious wedding ceremonies ; the girl is offered in marriage to the groom by her father or an appointed elderly relative.

Marriage by purchase in the original form , where the groom pays a bride-price (also known as bride-wealth), hereafter referred to in this book as "groom-dowry" prevails in many tribal societies and cultures in Africa, in some countries of Europe, China, Japan, India, and several Latin American countries, especially Peru.

There was a parallel evolution of what came to be called " bridal-dowry". The girl's father paid a price to the groom's family for accepting his daughter in marriage. This started as a natural inclination of a wealthy father out of love and affection for her daughter to assist the couple setting up a comfortable new household. But in many societies and countries where there was a gender imbalance, women outnumbering men, this tended to become a general practice. This form of marriage became widespread especially in Asian countries and is still prevalent in China, Japan, and India, among others.

In the modern Western societies, the dominant form of marriage is a variant of marriage by purchase. The modern wedding presents from the bride's family are a relic of the ancient form of marriage by purchase. In fact marriage is formalised by an exchange of gifts. It has become a custom for the bride's father " to acknowledge the bridegroom's payment with a return gift, which, as time went on, approximated more and more in value to the sum offered for the bride". In some wedding ceremonies even now (e.g., in Jewish wedding), bride's father gives a coin to the bridegroom as a symbolic payment (dower) to the groom for accepting her as his wife.

1.4 Monogamy and Polygamy

In the modern Western society and in most other parts of the world, both by law and longstanding tradition marriages are monogamous.

Polygamy

Polygamy (a man having several wives) from the same tribe appeared to be the most logical form of relationship in a tribal society, concerned with survival and preservation of the tribe. More wives meant more children. More wives and more children meant more helping hands on family farms. Secondly, men faced higher risks of dying early due to tribal warfare and hunting for food. The consequent excess of women was a compelling reason for polygamy. Women themselves often favored polygamy. It permitted them to nurse their children longer and therefore reduce the frequency of motherhood. (For a discussion of the evolution and changing roles of women, see Arun S. Roy, "Gender Roles", *International Encyclopedia of Social and Economic Policy*, Compiled by Nottinghill University, UK, Routledge Publishing (forthcoming).

In the patriarchal system, wives and children were economic assets for man. The more a man had of them, the richer he was considered to be. Several historians have quoted ancient folklores to show that the poor man practiced monogamy and it was usually the ambition of a primitive man to rise to the respected position of a polygamous male.

There is a popular belief that polygamy became a common practice with the emergence of Islam. Under the Islamic law, a man may legally have as many as four wives. This is a misconception. There is evidence to suggest that it prevailed many centuries ago for social and economic reasons. The Old Testament of the Bible describes the practice of polygamy among the ancient Hebrews. It is possible that the gender imbalance, women outnumbering men, became particularly acute due to incessant civil wars in the Arabian countries at the time of Prophet Mohammed. With a view to addressing the issues relating to the miserable plight of widowhood, polygamy received a particular encouragement from the religious and political leaders.

Historians attribute the gradual decline of polygamy to several factors.

First, the decrease in danger and violence, consequent upon a settled agricultural life brought the man and woman towards an approximate numerical equality.

Secondly, with greater gender balance, jealousy in the male and possessiveness in the female became important factors and polygamy remained the luxury of only the prosperous minority.

Thirdly, as wealth accumulated and rights of private property became stronger, inheritance and division of bequests became more complex. It became desirable to differentiate wives into "chief wife" and concubines, so that only the children of the former should be entitled to the legacy.

With the emergence of Christianity, in Europe monogamy became the lawful form of sexual association. During the late 19th century, the Christian church officially prohibited polygamy. Some small religious sects (e.g., Mormons) among the Christians in the U.S. still engage in plural relationships, in spite of the legal and religious sanction against it.

1.5 Polyandry

Polyandry (or a woman married to several men) has been found to be less common in human history. Here again gender imbalance seems to have been the main reason, though there are differences of opinion among anthropologists on this.

Polyandry has virtually disappeared but it is still found among some tribes that reside in the mountainous regions (e.g., Tibet, Sikkim and Bhutan and some parts of Assam in India, Peru and Columbia). The reason for this is not entirely clear. The form of their society is matriarchal. Women act as heads of households. Also, it is the daughters who have the first claim to property. In Tibet, a woman may marry the eldest son of a family and take his brothers as husbands also. This practice reduced competition among heirs and ensured minimal fragmentation of landed property.

1.6 Endogamy and Exogamy

The practice of marrying within one's clan or group is called *endogamy*. *Exogamy*, on the other hand, refers to marrying outside one's clan or group. Some religious faiths prohibit exogamy or marriage outside the religious group. For instance, in a Muslim marriage if one of the partners is a non-Muslim, he or she has to be converted first to Islam. The preferred form of marital relationship from time immemorial had been and continues to be endogamous. The definition and scope of endogamy varies across cultures and societies, however.

One rule that is virtually shared by all societies is the prohibition against incest---sexual relations between two biologically related male and female : mother and son, father and daughter, or brother and sister. In some countries and under some religious faiths, stepbrothers and stepsisters are not allowed to marry legally (e.g., U.K.). In ancient Egypt, however, brother-sister marriage and sexual relation was common in the royal family, probably to maintain the purity of the royal bloodline. In some Southern provinces of India, marriages between the niece and maternal uncle and between cousins are still not uncommon. The reason for this practice was presumably to preserve the property rights in a close knit family in a matriarchal society. For a detailed history of evolution of such marriages, see J. Puthenkalam, *Marriage and the Family in Kerala*, Monograph, Dept. of Sociology, University of Calgary, 1977.

As discussed later, there is a prohibition among the Hindus to marry within the same 'gotra' or clan, to discourage excessive in-breeding (MN-11). The possible reason for this is that marrying within the same gotra could lead to incestuous relations. There is a general consensus among biologists that such endogamous marriages on an extensive scale can lead to a deterioration in mental faculties of the successive generations of offsprings in the long run.

1.7 Marriage As A Social Contract

The ancient Greeks and Romans laid a great deal of stress on the religious ceremony and in order for a marriage to be recognized, it was required to be sanctified by the authority of the religious institution. This tradition has been generally maintained even to this day. But in many countries and societies marriage came to be considered as a social (legal) contract, and hence a religious ceremony was not essential.
Some historians point out that the French Revolution first proclaimed marriage to be a social contract rather than a religious one . This gave rise to marriage as a civil ceremony instead of a religious one. Yet the vast majority of marriages in the world today are formalised through a religious ceremony with all the trappings of elaborate rituals, festivities rather than simple civil ceremonies.
Also, it needs to be emphasized that over the last 30 years or so, a new phenomenon has emerged, namely, cohabitation by an adult man and an adult woman in the same household in the same way as a husband a wife would live together---commonly known as common law marriages. In recent years in the U.S. and Canada 30 to 40 percent are reported to be have lived together before marriage. In some legal jurisdictions, these are recognized as common law marriages if they have lived together for a certain number of years.

1.8 Same-Sex Marriages

The conventional definition of marriage emphasizes the union between a man and a woman, that is, between members of the opposite sex. Some people do not consider this to be comprehensive enough to include committed relationships between homosexuals that are often observed in modern times in case of individuals with a sexual orientation toward people of the same sex. Neither Christianity nor any other religion of the world recognizes a union of two individuals of the same sex as marriage. The reason for this is understandable. One of the goals of marriage was procreation for the preservation of human race. Religious conservatives fear that recognition of gay rights threatens the very sacred institution of marriage.

In North America such unions are not yet legally recognized as marriages but gay and human right activists are pushing for extending the pension and other benefits to same- sex partners. The movement to open civil marriage to same-sex couples achieved its first temporary success in 1993 with the decision of the Hawaii Supreme Court that the restriction of marriage to opposite-sex couples would be presumed unconstitutional unless the state could demonstrate that it furthered a compelling state interest. As a reaction to the Hawaii case, the federal Defense of Marriage Act (1996) provided that no state would be required to recognize a same-sex marriage from another state, and also defined marriage for federal-law purposes as opposite-sex.

In 2002 through 2004, courts in six Canadian provinces held that the opposite-sex definition of marriage was contrary to Canada's Charter of Rights. Canada is likely to legally recognize the same-sex marriage very shortly. If so, Canada would be the first English-speaking country to recognize same-sex marriages.

In 2001, the Netherlands became the first country to open civil marriage to same-sex couples. Belgium became the second in 2003. Same sex marriage partners are being accorded access to pension benefits, health insurance, and inheritance in many countries of Europe. In Europe the proportion of people living as same-sex partners is substantially higher than in USA and Canada.

For a discussion of issues relating to same-sex marriages, see Merin Yuval, *Equality for Same-Sex Couples : The Legal Recognition of Gay Partnerships in Europe and the United States*, Chicago : University of Chicago Press, 2002 ; Sean, Cahill, *Same-Sex Marriage in the United States: Focus on the Facts,*Rowman & Littlefield, 2004 ; Lynn D. Wardle et al (ed.), *Marriage and Same-Sex Unions: a Debate*, Praeger, 2003 ; Andrew Sullivan (ed.), *Same-Sex Marriage : Pro and Con : A Reader*, Vintage Books, 1997.

Chapter 2

Hinduism and Marriage

The Hindus are the third largest religious group in the world. The world population that practices the Hindu faith are estimated to be around 900 million (15%) out of a total world population of 6 billion. The population of the Christian faith is about twice that of the population of the Hindu faith (33%), followed by Muslims (18%).

Instead of footnotes, some details are placed at the end of the book under the title " Miscellaneous Notes" (MN---numbered).

2.1 The Essence and Salient Features of Hinduism

Wedding customs are derived from and are based on the religious beliefs and practices. For this reason, a few words by way of the Hindu religious philosophy would be relevant as a background.

First, Oldest Surviving Religion
> Hinduism is the oldest and most complex of the active religious faiths that are known to the world. Historians and archeologists have determined the age of Hinduism to be 5,000 to 6,000 years [MN-1].

Second, Hinduism More a Philosophy or Way of Life
> According to many, it is more appropriate to characterize Hinduism as a philosophy of life, a way of life than a religion. This is for several reasons :
> (a) Hinduism does not have a designated prophet as all other major religions have ;

(b) Hinduism does not have a single holy book or scripture like the Bible of the Christians, the *Book of Moses* of the Jews, the *Koran* of the Muslims, *Zend Avesta* of the Zoroastrians, or the *Guru Granth Sahib* of the Sikhs. The Hindu faith is, on the other hand, scattered in a variety of religious scriptures (Vedas [MN-8], Upanishads (MN-9), Bhagvat Gita [MN-10] and numerous other sources) ;

Third, Hinduism is mainly polytheistic

It is mainly polytheistic and it propagates the worship of a multiplicity of gods. But it also admits of monotheism, the worship of a single god. For instance, Shaivites who are mainly worshippers of Lord Shiva, or Vaishnavites who are mainly worshippers of Lord Vishnu also belong to the Hindu faith ;

Fourth, Hindus are mainly believers in image worship

Hindus are image worshippers unlike the Muslims. But Hinduism also recognizes and admits of the worship of god as the infinite and formless, as practiced by the followers of Brahmo Samaj and Arya Samaj.

Fifth, Hinduism is inclusive rather than exclusive.

As noted, Hinduism is not based on one single religious scripture. This does sometime pose a problem of consistency. But this makes Hinduism less rigid than other religions. Hinduism is known to be one of the most tolerant religions (Lewis Hopfe, *Religions of the World*) in terms of its basic philosophy [MN-21].

Sixth, three central pillars of the Hindu faith are :

- One, the material body is ephemeral and transitory, while the soul ('atman') is immortal [MN-18]
- Second, one's soul migrates from body to body (transmigration of soul or the theory of the cycle of birth and rebirth) according to past deeds ('karma') [MN-19]
- Third, the ultimate goal in life is attainment of liberation ('nirvana') through good deeds.

It is also worth noting that Hinduism has been the source of three other major religions of the world : Jainism, Buddhism, and Sikhism . All these three religions are the offshoots of the Hindu faith.

2.2 Sources of Hindu Wedding Customs

The Hindu wedding customs and rituals are derived from three different sources.

- The Vedas (*Rigveda* and *Atharva-Veda*). These are considered to go back to at least 3,500 years (1,500 B.C.).
- *Grihasutras* or domestic rituals and laws which go back to 500 B.C.
- *Dharmasastras* or *Samhitas* (notably *Manu-Samhita*, MN-15) go back to about 200 B.C. to 200 A.D.

The prescribed rituals and verses describing the customs differ slightly in these three sources. The rituals and customs described in the second source above, domestic rituals, had been influenced by changes in the social structure, political developments and contacts with Non-Aryan races. But there is a remarkable core of similarity among these.

In addition to these three sources, two epics of the Hindu religion, namely, *Ramayana* [MN-12] , and *Mahabharta* [MN-13] also shed some interesting light on the marriage customs in the ancient Indian society.

2.3 The Concept of Marriage and Hinduism

It is difficult to determine the time when the institution of marriage became established in India among the Hindus and followers of other religious faiths. Available accounts clearly indicate that marriage was an established institution during the Vedic times (at least 3,500 years ago).

Spiritual Union

It is evident from the earliest Vedic texts that Hindu marriage was *not a civil contract but a spiritual union of two souls* for their worldly happiness, propagation of the race, and for the development of the best qualities of human nature (Rigveda, X.85.42).

The foregoing leads to another distinctive feature of Hindu marriage, namely, its indissolubility in the eyes of the religious tradition [MN-6]. Many Vedic texts have emphasized that marriage is not a temporary union between a man and a woman for merely sexual gratification ; it is a permanent union of the husband and wife extending beyond the present births. The legality of an annulment or dissolution of a Hindu marriage was accorded only recently under The Hindu Marriage Act of 1955.

Hindu Rites and Rituals

According to the Vedas, a man's worldly life is regulated by rites and rituals from birth to death. Marriage is the most important of the of these rituals or rites ('samskaras'). Some of the others are : giving the child its name ('namakaran'), cutting the child's hair for the first time ('churakaran'), sacred thread ceremony for the Brahmin boy ('upanayan'), completion of studies ('snatak'), and funeral rites ('sraddha').

According to the Vedas, an unmarried daughter belongs to a supernatural being, Savitur, the Sun-god and her mortal father only acts as the custodian until she is married at which time she is given to her human husband for performing the wordly duties . As part of the wedding ceremony, several verses ('Mantras') are recited by the bride's father releasing the bride from the mortal father's household (Rigveda, X).

The earliest references to the institution of marriage in India are found in the Rigveda. A detailed description of the marriage ceremony of Surya and Soma is found in Rigveda X.85. Some of the verses that are recited in a present day Hindu wedding ceremony are the same as those that were written in the Rigveda thousands of years ago .

Meaning of Marriage

In the Hindu philosophy, marriage and marital duties occupy a very important place. Marriage is a sacrament in the sense that it is a religious duty.

Human life is divided into four phases : *Dharma* (righteusness), *Artha* (earning a livelihood to satisfy material needs), *Kama* (satisfying worldly desires), and *Moksha* (pursuit of liberation through religious rites). These phases are not necessarily in the same order. For the satisfaction of worldly desires living the experience of a householder is extremely important. Several scriptures declare that wife is the sole mistress of the household and it is she who renders a man complete and rightly she is to be regarded as half of his self [MN-25]. Further, the soul of a man who leads the life of a householder does not attain liberation unless he is married . An exception is in the case of a person who chooses the path of complete religious pursuit ('sannyasi').

In the classical Indian language , Sanskrit, several words are used interchangeably for marriage such as 'Vivah', 'Parinay', 'Upayama', 'Panigrahana" and "Udvaha' . The terms 'Vivah' and 'Udvah' literally mean to carry and are derived from the root 'Vaha'. According to scholars it refers to the fact that after the union of hands of the two, they are carried by a chariot to the bridegroom's home. 'Panigrahan' means accepting the hands of the maiden as one's wife. The essential idea underlying marriage is that the woman is offered in marriage and man accepts her as his wife.

The idea that an unmarried woman is under the guardianship of her father and has to be formally offered in marriage is not unique to Hindu scriptures. The same idea is to be found in the Christian and Jewish faiths, for instance.

2.4 Forms of Marriage in Hinduism

The ancient Hindu scriptures mention eight forms of marriage of which the following four are mentioned below [MN-23]:

- Marriage with consent of the bride's father (*brahma* marriage)

The bride's father invites the groom after negotiation to marry the   daughter. Gifts in the form of a dowry are given to the groom to help set up a new household. The marriage was to be solemized by a priest according to the Vedic rites.

- Marriage by Purchase (*asura* marriage)
  Money is given to the parents of the girl and was considered as prohibited as it meant sale of the bride.

- An elopement or secret marriage *(gandharva* marriage)
  This form of marriage was a taboo as mating without solemnising had   no place in the Hindu code of ethics .

- Marriage by Force (*rakshasha* marriage)
  This form of marriage was also not recognized as ethical.

A special form of 'gandharva' marriage was the self-choice of the groom by the bride (*sawamvar*). The Hindu law books laid down that if a girl was not married by her parents soon after attaining puberty, she was allowed to choose her own husband but this was to be done in a public congregation and it was to be solemnised by a religious ceremony [MN-24]. The 'Brahma' form of marriage was considered to be the most acceptable form of marriage and it still continues to be so [MN-11].

The Vedic texts and the domestic laws prescribed in great details the duties of a householder, rights and privileges of the husband and wife, duties of a father toward his daughter, acceptable and forbidden types of marriage, marriage and other rites and rituals, desirable qualities of the bride and bridegroom, etc. For detailed discussions of the marriage customs and rituals prescribed in the Vedic texts, see A. B. Keith, *The Religion and Philosophy of the Veda and Upanishads*, Vol. II, Chapter 21.

Chapter 3

The Hindu Wedding Ceremony

In contrast to the Western societies and religions, wedding ceremonies and customs followed by families of the Hindu faith are much more elaborate and these vary widely. This chapter focuses on the most commonly observed practices and traditions. Diversities are described in the subsequent chapter.

3.1 A Typical Hindu Wedding

For reasons that are discussed below, a Hindu wedding ceremony is quite extensive and elaborate. It differs from region to region and even from family to family, depending upon local customs and traditions. The following is a brief description of some of the common wedding customs and ceremonies. These are based on the Rigveda which is believed to be at least 3,500 years old.

1.Engagement and Bretrothal (*Ashirvad / Mangni*)
In the engagement ceremony which precedes the actual wedding by anywhere from six months to a couple of days, boy's father and /or relatives visit the daughter's house and present a piece of jewellery to the girl as a token of their commitment. This is followed by a visit by some elders from the girl's side to bless the future bridegroom. Based upon the astronomical calendar, an auspicious day and time for the wedding ceremony is determined.
2. Ceremonial Bath (*Haldi Snan*)
On the wedding day, in the respective houses of the bride and groom, the relatives and friends conduct ceremonial baths of the bride and groom with oil and turmeric paste (also called 'Mangalsnan'/'Gaye Halud' ceremony). The groom and the bride are expected not to go outside of the respective houses except to the wedding hall.
3. Wedding Procession (*Barat*)

As the groom's wedding procession arrives at the bride's house, the groom is welcome by the mother-in-law and other family members and friends.

4. Offerings to Deities (*Puja*)

At the wedding hall especially decorated with colorful fresh flowers and design, the priest welcomes the congregation, and the Vedic gods and goddesses are invoked. Also, ancestors of the bride and bridegroom's families are invoked and their blessings are solicited by the priest and Vedic hymns specially composed for the special occasion are chanted.

5. Giving Away of the Bride (*Kanya-Daan*)

The bride's father or a designated elderly family member bestows the daughter to the groom in marriage.

6. Fire Ritual (*Lajahoma* or *Havan*)

A ceremonial fire is lit and fire god is invoked to witness the ceremony and give blessings.

7. Exchanging Garlands (*Jaimala* and *Panigrahan*)

With fire as the witness, the bride and groom exchange garlands and hold one another's hands and symbolically accept one another as the husband and wife.

8. Seven Steps or Vows (*Sapta-padi*)

This is the most important part of the wedding ceremony, socially and legally. The couple takes seven steps and takes vows for their mutual conjugal love and happiness.

9. Vermillion Mark (*Sindur Daan*)

As a mark of the married status, the groom puts vermillion mark on the bride's forehead.

10. Departure for the groom's home (*Vidai*)

The day after the wedding, the bride departs for the groom's home.

11. Wedding Reception and In-house Honeymoon (*Suhag Raat*)

In a reception at the groom's house, the new bride is formally introduced to the family and friends. The couple's room is specially decorated with fresh flowers and fragrances for them to spend a romantic night together when the marriage is consummated.

3.2 Wide Variations in Customs and Traditions

- India is more than a nation and less than a continent. Languages people speak, dresses they wear, food they eat and social customs and traditions they follow change as one travels every 400 or 500 miles in India. There is a wide variation of wedding customs and traditions even though they all may belong to the Hindu faith. These customs and traditions vary by family background, by region of residence, and by rural and urban society.
- The Hindu wedding ceremonies can be split up into two parts : 'sacramental' and 'popular customs'.
- The sacramental part is the core religious ceremony in which the presence of a priest is mandatory. The variations are relatively small in this respect.

There are at least two customs or rituals that are commonly found irrespective of the family background or place residence : *Agni* (or fire-god) being invoked as the witness of the union of the man and woman ; and *Sapta-padi*(or seven steps and vows) that are derived from the Hindu scripture, Rigveda.

Instead of footnotes, some details are placed at the end of the book under the title " Miscellaneous Notes" (MN---numbered).

Local Customs

With respect to the popular or local customs ('lokachar'), the presence of a priest is not necessary. It is with respect to these popular wedding customs that wide variations are found.

- The reason for variations in wedding customs is largely historical. India had been invaded from time to time by other races including the Greeks, Huns, and Mongols. The Indian way of life including dress, food habits and culture has been influenced by these foreign races. Wedding rites are no exception to this. To the basic Vedic rites which are written, various local customs have been added and adopted from time to time. These have often become an essential part of a wedding ceremony. For this reason, the wedding customs followed in Northern India , which was more vulnerable to foreign invasions , are somewhat different from those followed in South India. For geographic reasons, South India was well protected from these invasions and influences. It may also be noted in parentheses that as many foreign races settled down in India and lived there for centuries, the local Hindu culture and customs were also absorbed by them [MN-27].

Elaborate Rituals

The Hindu wedding rituals and customs are quite elaborate and extensive, as already mentioned. It may be important to emphasize the following in this context :

- One reason for such elaborate and extensive wedding rituals is that these rituals have been described in some details in the Vedas. Wedding rituals have not been laid down in such details in scriptures of other religions.
- Second, the prescribed rituals have religious overtones. All god-fearing families are eager to follow them to the letter lest the life of the newly married be marred by misfortune due to any irregularities.
- Third, in the Hindu religion, the ceremonies and festivities are symbolic. Rituals are observed to the letter even until today.
- Finally, as already mentioned above, Hindu wedding rituals have religious overtones. An essential component of the Hindu philosophy is the theory of the transmigration of the soul---the concept of immortality of the soul and cycle of birth and rebirth. Being fearful of the primitive idea of the evil spirit bringing bad luck, not only traditional gods and goddesses are invoked, but several generations of the bride

and bridegroom are invoked by name and clan ('gotra', MN-11) and their blessings are solicited. It is believed that their forefathers observe the ceremony from the other world and bestow their blessings. This also adds to the length of the ceremony.

3.3   Some General Customs

Engagement

Even at the risk of a sweeping generalization, arranged marriages (i.e., parents play a major role in the selection of of partners in marriage) are more common in the rural societies and cultures. In the urban societies and cultures, on the other hand, parents play a less important role.

In ancient India, it was at once the parents' religious responsibility (*dharma*) as well as the pleasure to arrange their daughter's or son's marriage. Contacts between a boy's and girl's families were established by relatives and family priests who often acted as matchmakers.

The parents would weigh the compatibility of the bride's and bridegroom's education, personal nature, tastes, and their family traditions and background. Caste also played and still does play an important part in the decision-making process, although intermarriage between castes is becoming more common in modern times, and especially so in urban societies.

After the parents on the two sides feel convinced that the boy and the girl would make a happy couple, they would proceed to formalise the betrothal with a short ceremony in the presence of friends and relatives. A feast follows. This is known in Bengal as *paka- dekha, or ashirvad , and mangni* in Punjab.

With the passage of time the way the bride and groom are selected has changed somewhat. In recent times, matrimonial advertisements in newspapers and more recently in the Internet have become quite common.

In the olden days boys and girls did not see one another before wedding (in very olden days, of course). Now, even in marriages where parents play some important role , courtship is accepted. With the spread of education among women, and girls no longer being confined to the four walls of the home, in enlightened families, girls have almost as much say in their marriage as boys.

In the engagement ceremony which precedes the actual wedding by anywhere from six months to a couple of days, boy's father and /or relatives visit the daughter's house and present a piece of jewellery to the girl as a token of their commitment. This is followed by a visit by some elders from the girl's side to bless the future bridegroom.

Selection of Auspicious Time

Before the marriage is finalised, it is common in Hindu marriages to compare the horoscopes of the bride and bridegroom for compatibility. Also, it is believed that the position of the stars influences the event and the priests determine an auspicious time for wedding [MN-5]. There are some months that are considered to be particularly auspicious and there are others that are not recommended for wedding ceremonies [MN-26].

Ceremonial Bath

On the wedding day in the morning, a ceremony is held both at the bride's and the groom's houses. This is called 'Gatraharidra' in Sanskrit and other popular local names are 'Gaye Halud' (Bengal), 'Mangal Snan'(Bihar), 'Mangal Snanam'(Tamil Nadu), 'Haldi Snan' (U.P.), and 'Vatna' (Punjab).

In villages, it is considered to be an elaborate, joyful and fun-filled event. The bride is escorted to a nearby river by a large crowd of friends and relatives to the accompaniment of music. The participants sing bridal songs (see Haldi Songs in a later chapter). The priest sanctifies the water for the bath of the bride. The water is mixed with perfume, turmeric and oil.

The ceremonial bath has a spiritual significance. Becoming united in marriage means union of the two bodies and two souls. The human bodies need to be purified before they are united in matrimony. The ceremonial bath is meant to make the bodies enter into a new phase of life ----of pleasure but also of duties and responsibilities of a householder. The Vedic verses which are prescribed for recitation by the priest indicate that it is meant to ward off evil spirits as they enter a very important phase of life.

The Apala Legend

Some Vedic scholars have also adduced in this context to the Apala legend described in the Rigveda (VIII. 91.7). Legend has it that the marriage negotiation of a girl named Apala was concluded after which she became afflicted by a terrible and incurable skin disease. Her young and beautiful body became deformed and ugly. She was carrying a curse from her previous birth. Apala became unmarriageable. In frustration she renounced the material world and spent many years to the worship of Indra. God Indra was pleased with her devotion and asked her to take a ceremonial bath. She regained her body and was endowed with eternal youth and beauty. The signifcance of turmeric is not so clear. To the best of knowledge of the present author, in the Vedic texts there is no reference to turmeric paste in the ceremonial bath and yet turmeric is used universally in Hindu marriages. It seems that the use of turmeric evolved as a custom in the post-Vedic times and became a part of the tradition. In indigenous Indian medicine, turmeric has a therapeutic property---it is often prescribed as a painkiller and is used for minor burns and cuts and also used as a cosmetic. The bride in the bride's house and the groom in the groom's house are bathed in water mixed with turmeric paste, oil, and perfume. Friends and relatives bestow their blessings----"may your new married life be free from pain and it be bright and beautiful like turmeric paste".

Wedding Procession

On the day of wedding , the bridegroom's party proceeds to the bride's house in the evening. A Hindu wedding would always be after the nightfall. Traditionally it is never solemnised during daytime, with minor exceptions in some communities (discussed in the next chapter).

In Punjab, Delhi, Rajasthan, and Himachal Pradesh, the bridegroom traditionally goes on a horseback in a procession. In the modern urban society, a luxurious car decorated with fresh flowers often takes the place of a horse. He is accompanied by a large number of friends and relatives with a group of musicians and dancers.

The custom of bridegroom going with a large party and on horseback seems to be a Persian influence---in Iran and several other Arab countries the groom still goes on a camel or horseback with a horde of musicians and dancers.

Members of the bridegroom's marriage party and other invited guests are entertained with sumptuous food depending upon the financial condition and social status. In small villages, almost the entire village is invited to the festivity and the feast. It is not uncommon in cases for the bride's family to run into huge debt for such large marriage expenses resulting from the social pressure. In recent years, some social organizations and religious groups have initiated steps in rural poor communities to arrange mass marriages with a view to reducing such costs.

Fasting

The main participants in this ceremony-- bride, bridegroom, and their fathers (or deputed elders in their absence) have to be on fast for the wedding day until the ceremony has been completed.

Among other possible reasons, in most Hindu ceremonies and forms of image worship, food and flowers are offered to the Divine. As a worshipper, one should eat and drink only after offerings have been made to the deity.

A traditional Hindu marriage is a religious ceremony. Rituals include making offerings of food and flowers to the deity and to the forefathers.

Fasting is commonly observed in many other religious ceremonies but probably for different reasons [MN-16].

3.4 Four Part Preliminary Ceremony

In the evening of the wedding day, bride's relatives and friends decorate the bride with sandalwood paste, fine jewellery and clothing. In some states such as Punjab, Delhi, and Rajasthan hands and feet of the bride are tattooed with Mehndi, a colorant made of plants and vegetables. This is certainly a Muslim influence on the Hindu wedding customs. This is not observed among the Hindu families in the Southern or the Eastern States of India. Historically they had much less contact with the Muslims than the Northern States of Punjab and U.P.

Wedding takes place in the house of the bride or a in place specially rented for the purpose. A traditional wedding ceremony can take 3 to 4 hours to be completed.

The wedding rituals can be divided into 4 parts :
1. Preliminary benedictions
2. Address by the minister (Priest) to the guests
3. Reception of of the bridegroom by the bride's father/bestower
4. Women's Rites

1. Preliminary benedictions(*Subharambha*)

A well known verse recited as part of this initiating ceremony is 'Gayatri Mantra' :

Om. tat Savitur varenyam
bhargo devasya dhimahi ;
dhiyo yo nah prachodayat.

(Om. We meditate upon the adorable Glory of God, the Shining One, the Creator: may He direct our thoughts.)

"Om" is a common word used as part of many Sanskrit Mantras (hymns). There is more than one interpretation of the word. There is a large consensus among the scholars that

'Om' is an expression of salutation to the divine spirit. According to one legend, Brahma (Lord of Creation) woke up from his long meditation and uttered the sound "Om" and the entire cosmos resonated with this sound and the world was created. The Om sound originated from the navel and was breathed out through the nostrils by Brahma. For this reason, it is also called Brahmanad.

Ancient teachers of yoga recommended the uttering of this sound for meditation. The modern medical opinion in the West has confirmed the therapeutic value of this sound structure.

Invoking Elements of Nature

According to Hindu scriptures, there are five elements of Nature which are life-giving (*panchabhut*) and after the death of the mortal body, it is believed that life returns to the five elements. These five elements are —earth ('khsiti'), water ('op'), sun ('tej'), air('morut'), and sky('baum', ether). Gods and goddesses representing these five elements as well as some other Vedic gods and goddesses are invoked for their blessings.

Earth (soil) is an essential ingredient in almost all Hindu ceremonies—symbolic of the tribute to and blessing from the Mother Earth. The evolution of this ritual can be traced to the age-old Aryan tradition of worshipping Nature and trying to live in harmony with it. Similarly, grass constitutes an essential ingredient in many religious festivals —symbolic of wealth and prosperity , a gift of Mother Nature. This is clearly understandable in an agrarian society that was highly dependent upon Nature for sustenance. Offerings to fire in almost all religious festivals and ceremonies including wedding also symbolise propitiating another element of Nature. The Hindus who are believed to be descendants of the Aryans were fire-worshippers, and so were the Zoroastrians of Persia (now Iran).

Invoking Gods and Goddesses

Every religious ceremony including wedding starts with the worship of Ganesh or Ganapati (the elephant-headed Hindu God). It is believed that Lord Ganesh is a great problem-solver and removes barriers to success (Remover of All Obstacles). Also important in a wedding ceremony is Narayana and offerings are made to Him as well.

In the Hindu mode of worship, gods and goddesses are divine beings but they also have human attributes, resembling to some extent the Greek mythology. Fruits and sweets are offered as food. They are offered water for drinking. They are also offered new clothing for wearing and perfumed water for taking bath. They are offered flowers as a mark of reverence. The Vedic verses that are recited at the wedding ceremony refer to these offerings.

Invoking the Ancesters

In addition to the gods and goddesses, ancesters of the groom and bride are also invoked on this occasion and their blessings for starting a new family that would lead to the growth of the race are solicited . For this reason, the ceremony is called 'Vriddhi Sraaddha', Vriddhi meaning growth, and the word 'Sraaddha' is a derivative of 'Shroddha' meaning respect.

Initiating the forefathers and asking for their blessings is also called 'Nandimukh' or 'Nandimukh Sraaddha'.

The ancestors are offered the same types of food and flowers as are offered to the gods and goddesses. Since one of the central tenets of the Hindu philosophy is immortality of the soul, it is believed that the forefathers observe this ceremony from the other world and bestow their blessing on the new couple. For details see K. L. Seshagiri Rao, *The concept of 'sraddha' in the Brahmanas, Upanisads*, Ph.D. Thesis, Harvard University, 1971.

2. Address by the Priest to the guests *(Purohit- Abhyagata-Samlap)*

The priest recites several verses welcoming the guests , stating the purpose of the gathering and soliciting their blessings and good wishes for the bride and the bridegroom who are about to get married.

3. Reception of the bridegroom by the bride's father/bestower *(Varswagatam)*

The priest asks the bride's father or the guardian to repeat after him a couple of verses addressing the groom by way of welcoming him to the house who sits in front of him.

4. Women's Rites (*Stri-achar*)

This is a non-Vedic rite and largely evolved as folk customs. There are no Vedic verses for these. There are two such women's rites that are very common. These are formal acceptance ('Varan') and auspicious meeting of eyes ('Shubho-Dristi').

4 (A) Formal Acceptance

After the bridegroom has agreed to marry, he puts on the clothes presented to him, and is taken to the inner part of the house. There the bride's mother performs the acceptance *(Varan)* ceremony. The bride's mother touches the groom's forehead, chest and his knees with a brass tray. The tray contains some 24 items which include paddy, soil, flowers, perfume, conch-shell, and turmeric which are considered to be auspicious objects and are believed to ward off evil.

4(B) Auspicious Meeting of Eyes

This practice is particularly popular in Bengal. The bride is seated on a decorated wooden seat and she is carried by the male relatives in the centre of the gathering. She is circled around the standing bridegroom seven times and garlands are exchanged seven times (*malyadaan* or *mala badal*). There is no hymn for this in the Vedic texts. The bride and groom are unable to see another as their eyes remain covered with a veil and strings of flowers respectively.

This developed as a popular Hindu wedding custom in the post-Vedic times. Some scholars see this as a wish expressed by the bride and bridegroom at the time of exchanging garlands,

" May we be born seven times on this earth as the husband and wife".

After this, a cloth awning is spread over the heads of the bride and bridegroom . They secretly exchange glances (*subha-dristi*). In olden days when marriages were arranged by the father , that was the first time that the bride and bridegroom saw one another.

3.5 Main Wedding Ceremony

This consists of the following six parts :
    (i)Bestowal of the bride (*Kanya-Daan*)
    (ii)Holding of the palm (*Pani-grahan*)
    (iii)Stepping on the stone slab (*Shilarohan)*
    (iv)Fire ritual (*Kushandika/ Lajahoma)*
    (v)Seven steps (*Sapta-padi)*
    (vi) Address to the Pole Star (*Dhruva Darshan)*
    (vii) Vermillion Mark (*Sindur Daan)*

(i) Bestowal of the bride

In the process of bestowal of the bride in marriage to the bridegroom, the bride's father/relative , utters a variety of Sanskrit verses. Following is the substance the verses :

"In the presence of Lord Vishnu, today , after welcoming you , I so-and-so bestow upon you so-and-so in marriage as the bride so-and-so."

The groom offers his prayers to the Lord of Love (Kama) and asks for his blessings. The priest ties the corners of the bride and groom's scarf ends with 'haritaki' fruits signifying that they are tied to each other for ever (knot-tying).
Bestowal of the daughter by the father with the underlying implication that she has to be offered is not unique to the Hindu wedding ceremony. In all religious faiths including the Christian and Jewish, an unmarried daughter remains under the care and guardianship of the father, and she has to be offered by him in marriage . This is a relic of the distant past and some modern feminists find this objectionable.

(ii) Holding the bride's palm

The bridegroom gives the bride a couple of clothes and holds her hand. He recites [MN-7],

" I hold your hand for a happy married life and with me you may attain old age. God, in His various manifestations has given you to me for household duties".

(iii)Stepping on stone slab

A flat slab of stone is placed near the couple. The bride places her right foot on the slab and the bridegroom says,

"I place upon the lap of the divine earth, an auspicious and firm stone for you, for the sake of progeny and our long life."

The stone is a symbol of firmness and is intended to confirm marital fidelity. According to some social historians this may have its origin in the ancient custom of oath-taking on a stone. When the Romans chose a military leader, they were required to stand on a stone and proclaim their loyalty to the new military leader.

(iv) Fire ritual (*Laja-homa*)

A fire is kindled in front of the couple with wood chips and is enclosed with bricks. The bridegroom stands behind the bride and holds her two palms with his. They offer puffed rice as an offering to the fire –god (the ceremony is called 'Lajahoma' in Sanskrit).
The bride recites ,

> " May my husband live long. May he live a hundred years."

The bridegroom recites,

> "This girl is going to her husband's home from her parents' home . With your blessing may we be able to remove all evil-doers".

Offering made to fire is an important part of most Hindu ceremonies including wedding. Fire is the witness of this marriage . What is the significance of the fire ? In the Vedic rituals fire has been considered to be a major god having the power of destroying the evil spirits with its heat and light. This is also common among the Zoroastrians, fire worshippers.

(v) Seven steps (Vows)

The bride and bridegroom take seven steps or vows together as they circle the fire. The fire must be circled clockwise to signify moving with time and not against it. With white rice paste seven little circles are made around the fireplace . The bride steps forward and places her right foot within each circle one after the other. The groom accompanies her holding her hand. At each step, the bridegroom recites the following verses and the bride repeats the same. The groom recites,

"With god's blessings, we take the seven steps to married life".

These seven steps are believed to be prayer to seven sages of ancient India, 'Saptarshi' [for the Sanskrit text see MN-3].

Step one : *May the Lord lead us to happiness.*

Step two : *May the Lord lead us to prosper together.*

Step three : *May we help each other in fulfilling our duties in life.*

Step four : *May God help us to share each other's company in happiness and sorrow alike.*

Step five : *May we be kind to all living beings.*

Step six : *May we find in each other the true meaning of life.*

Step seven : *May we join each other in the pursuit of life's highest goals.*

"You are my friend in life through these seven steps. May I attain your friendship and may your friendship unite me with you for eternity" [MN-4].

It is believed that these seven vows with fire-god as the witness bind the bride and the groom in an eternal bond which goes beyond the current birth.

After the couple has taken the seven vows, they together pray to the Creater of the cosmos (Brahma) and the Protector of the universe (Vishnu) :

"may our married life be endowed with health, happiness and grant of progeny and may we grow old together".

An important mantra uttered by the two separately is the following :

Om. yadetat hridayam tava
tadastu hridayam mama ;
yadidam hridayam mama
tadastu hridayam tava.

(Om. This, which is your heart, may it be my heart; and this, which is my heart, may it be your heart.)

This is a beautiful verse signifying the union of the hearts and souls of a man and a woman in an eternal bond. Although the expression is not to be found in the Rigveda, this part of the ceremony is usually described as 'Hriday Sparshan' (Touching the Hearts).

Seven Ceremonial Lamps

There is a local custom in some Eastern provinces of India that as each of the seven steps is taken by the couple, friends of the bride stand nearby and each one lights a ceremonial lamp. These lamps are kept lighted until the sunrise.
Sapta-padi in the presence of ceremonial fire is considered to be the very essence of the Hindu wedding ceremony, even if other minor ceremonies are not performed.
The Hindu Marriage Act of 1955 states that for a marriage to be legally recognized as a Hindu marriage with all the implied rights and privileges, Sapta-padi is essential. It says, " ...with Sapta-padi, that is, the taking of seven steps by the bride and the bridegroom jointly before the sacred fire, the marriage becomes complete and binding when the seventh step is taken". However, it also states that if any Hindu does not recognize a ritual such as Sapta-padi as essential, any other form is considered as a marriage if the intention of the marriage can be shown to be present.

(vi) Address to the Pole Star

The religious wedding ceremony ends with the couple's address to the Pole Star ('Arundhati'). The special significance of the pole star is that it eternally remains fixed in the constellation according to the ancient Hindu astronomy. The bride utters a mantra which says—

Om. dhruvam asi dhruvaham patikule bhuayasam

(Oh star dhruva (Arundhati), as you are fixed for ever, may I be fixed in my husband's family.)

(vii) Vermillion Mark

The bridegroom puts vermillion ('sindur') on the bride's forehead between the two eyebrows as well as in the parting of the hair as the mark of a married woman. The bride's mother or a female elderly relative gives an iron bangle and a bangle made of conch shell to the bride to wear.

The use of vermilion mark is a symbol of marriage in most Hindu communities as a ring is in most marriages in the Western society and Christian marriages in particular.

Among some tribals of India, mere putting the vermillion mark by the boy on the forehead of the girl in the presence of some invited guests constitutes a valid marriage.

What is the significance of the vermillion mark ? One speculation is that it evolved as a custom in India but it is not unique in India. It presumably has an association with red colour. It signifies defloration, that is, taking away a woman's virginity. Dr. E. Westermarck, a well known researcher on marriage customs in the world mentioned that in Greece and Rome, it was customary to cover the bed of the newly married couple with red bedsheet. Similarly in China, even to this day good wishes are written on red papers and suspended on the top of the nuptial bed.

At the end the priest and others congratulate and bless the new couple and this concludes the wedding ceremony. The priest recites the following Vedic verse and the gathering is requested to repeat after him :

"Om. Be an Empress over your father-in-law, and be an Empress over your mother-in-law. Be an Empress over the sisters of your husband, and an Empress also over his brothers." [MN-17]

Kissing of the bride and the groom as is seen at the conclusion of the Christian wedding ceremony is not seen in a Hindu wedding ceremony. Neither is kissing common in the Islamic ceremony. Unlike traditional Christian and Jewish marriages, in traditional Hindu marriages there is no written marriage contract or certificate which can be used as an evidence of marriage. This often creates problems in a court of law . To resolve this, sometimes the bride and groom get legally married and obtain a marriage certificate before or after the traditional marriage ceremony.

3.6 Miscellaneous Customs

- Mangal-sutram (Bridal Thread)

Vedic verses are usually followed in all parts of India in Hindu wedding. Either in addition to the above or as a substitute for some rituals such as vermillion ceremony mentioned above, the bride is offered what is called *Mangal-sutram* (in some places also called *Tali* in the local language). This custom is not found in the Vedas and there are no mantras for this specific ceremony. This is comparable with the ring exchanging ceremony in Western marriages.
The custom is obligatory in the southern provinces of Tamil Nadu, Maharashtra, Andhra Pradesh, and Kerala. No marriage is complete without this and this concludes the wedding. It is not customary in Bengal, Bihar, Assam, Punjab, or Rajasthan.
Mangal-sutram is a necklace made of black and golden beads with variations in design. The bridegroom places this necklace around the wife's neck and it is symbolic of the bridegroom's acceptance of his sacred duties towards her as the husband as long as he lives. So long as her husband is living, 'mangal-sutram' is the most precious symbol of her married status in society.

- Departure for the Groom's Home

Usually the day after wedding some minor women's rites are performed and she leaves her paternal home for the husband's.

In the husband's home, the new bride is initiated into the kitchen and on a convenient day, a wedding reception is arranged where the new bride is introduced to the husband's family and friends.

- Honeymoon

The Western style honeymoon is becoming popular in the Indian sub-continent and the couple leaves after wedding for a vacation. The traditional style honeymoon for consummation of marriage is at the groom's house. A bedroom is decorated with flowers and the new couple spends the night together for the first time. It is variously called the flower-night (*phool sajya* in Bengal), and love-night (*suhag raat* in the Punjab and other Northern provinces).

- The Ramayana Legend

In many parts of Bihar and U.P., on the wedding night the newly-wed husband makes a wide circle with rice paste and the new bride spends the night within this circle. Nearby the bridegroom is kept awake the rest of the night and keeps a watch on the bride. Usually the bridegroom's friends and relatives keep him amused with amorous songs, jokes and conversation. At the sunrise , the bride comes out of the circle . The bridegroom holds the bride's hand and renews his marriage pledge, " Our bond is eternal and will go from life to life. I pledge that I will always be with you and protect you from the demons and evil spirits." The custom evidently originated from the Ramayana legend.
According to story of the Ramayana, Lord Rama was tricked by his stepmother to spend 14 years in a forest incognito. One day his beautiful wife Sita saw a golden deer and wanted to have it captured but it ran away. When Rama went after the deer, he asked his brother, Laxman, to look after his wife, Sita until his return. A little later they heard a human voice asking for help. Getting concerned that Rama 's life was in danger, Sita requested her brother-in-law to go to his rescue but he was reluctant to leave Sita alone in the cottage. When Sita insisted, he left to answer the call for rescue but made a circle and asked Sita not to go out of that circle. After he left,

demon Ravana came to the cottage in human form and begged for food. Sita was reluctant to cross the boundary of the circle but when the beggar insisted, she crossed the boundary and Ravana forcibly ran away with Sita.

- Tree-Marriages (*Briksha-Vivah*)

In ancient times, tree-marriage ('briksha-vivah') was a common custom. It has survived to this day in many villages in some parts of Punjab, Bihar, Rajasthan, and Himachal Pradesh. According to some religious sects, finding a bridegroom for one's daughter was the sacred duty of the father and a failure to do that was considered as committing an unpardonable sin. In a society in which warfare was common and mortality among young men who went to war was high, girls outnumbered men. This gave rise to the practice of tree-marriage.
An unmarried girl for whom a suitable match had not been found as she reached the age of puberty, she would be married to a tree with the usual pomp and grandeur. This marriage could later be annulled in the event a real marriage was negotiated.
According to another custom, a man marrying for the third time had to be first married to a tree. Third wife was believed to bring bad luck so that the third wife would actually count as his fourth.

- Dulha Deo

Among the Dravidian people, Dulha Deo is considered to be the god of marriage. Legend has it that when Dulha Deo was going on horseback to fetch his wife from his father-in-law's house, on the way a lightning struck turning him and the horse into stone. Some Dravidian people make offerings of milk and goatmeat to Dulha Deo and Thunder to propitiate them and ask for their blessings.

- Pitcher Marriage (*Kumbha-vivah*)

In a traditional Hindu family, horoscopes of the boy and girl are usually compared although the importance of this is gradually declining. If the astrologers do not agree that it is an auspicious match, the girl is first married to a well decorated pitcher before the actual wedding. This custom is more commonly found in villages and is known as 'Kumbha-vivah'.

Chapter 4

Some Regional Variations In Hindu Marriage Ceremony

As already noted, details of the wedding ceremony and customs differ across various communities and regions in India, even though they may all belong to the Hindu faith. Besides the religious tradition, a community may differ by province of residence and the language they speak, which define certain cultural characteristics of the group. In this chapter some interesting and notable variations around the customs and traditions described in the preceding chapter are discussed . Some repetitions are inevitable. Readers who do not want to get into too many details, may like to skip this chapter.

> Instead of footnotes, some details are placed at the end of the book under the title " Miscellaneous Notes" (MN---numbered).

4.1 Marriage Patterns : North and South

An interesting difference in the patterns of marriage relationships between the northern and southern parts India may be emphasized. Broadly, in the Indo-Aryan-speaking north, a family seeks marriage alliances with people to whom it is not already linked by ties of blood. In the Dravidian-speaking south, on the other hand, a family seeks to strengthen existing kin ties through marriage, preferably with blood relatives.

In South India, marriages are preferred between cousins (especially cross-cousins, that is, the children of a brother and sister) and even between uncles and nieces (especially a man and his elder sister's daughter). The principle involved is that of return--the family that gives a daughter expects one in return, if not now, then in the next generation. The main reason for such marriage customs is that the property and wealth remain within a closed family. The effect of such marriages is to bind people together in relatively small, tight-knit kin groups (for more details, see Irawati Karve, *Kinship Organization in India*, 1968).

4.2 Decoration of the Marriage Hall

Marriage Halls (*Vivah Mandap/Manch*) are tastefully decorated with fresh flowers and with beautiful designs and motifs.

In Bengal, Orissa, and several States of the South India, earthen or metallic pitchers are placed at the entrance. The pitcher is filled with water. No life can be sustained without water. Water is life force . The significance of the pot filled with water is symbolic of the wish that the special occasion be full with life force.

Quite often a whole coconut or a stem with mango leaves ('Amra Pallav')is placed at the top of the pitcher. Mango leaves probably are symbolic of youthfulness. A variation of the pitcher is found in Kerala where it is filled with unhusked rice and a banana flower is placed in the middle of the pitcher. Rice is a symbol of wealth and prosperity. These pitchers are also artistically decorated.

Rice paste is used to decorate the floors. This is called 'Alpona' in Bengal and 'Rangoli' in some other regions. Lotus has a special significance in the Hindu mythology. Lotus as a symbol of purity, and lamp as a symbol of light and wisdom are commonly used in these decorations. Lotus and ceremonial lamp have a special significance in the Buddhist ceremonies as well, as mentioned later.

In Bengal and Orissa, designs of fish figure prominently as a symbol of fertility.

It has become a tradition to play the Indian flute (Shehnai) on this occasion. The shehnai music adds to the festive ambiance.

4.3 Wedding Dress

In contrast to the bridal dresses used in the Western countries, the bridal dresses are usually very bright and colourful. The wedding traditional dresses vary by region and local customs. A detailed description of how the wedding dresses differ across the various

States of India is beyond the scope of this book. The following would serve as some examples :

- It is customary in a Bengali Hindu wedding for the bride to wear a colourful 'Benarasi' sari, traditionally a red one. In Eastern culture and especially in the Hindu tradition, for women the colour red is symbolic of love and romance. The groom wears a fine dhoti and silk kurta. The Bengali bride and bridegroom wear crowns ('topor') specially made for the occasion.

- A Punjabi bride's traditional dress consists of a bright red salwar kameez or an elaborately embroidered sari. She wears a variety of jewellery, especially long ear-rings or 'balis' and a wide necklace. The red and white bangles made of ivory and bone are a must for the Punjabi bride.

- In a Malayali Hindu wedding the bride wears the traditional two piece sari, called *Mundu*, or any other coloured sari except black. The preferred colour is off-white or cream usually having a border. The groom is usually clad in a dhoti and *angavastram*.

- The traditional Rajasthani Hindu wedding dress is bright red in colour. The jewellery consists of the *rakhri* (a circular piece of jewellery for the forehead), danglers for the ears, the *timaniyaan* (a choker studded with uncut diamonds) the *chooda* (a set of ivory and gold bangles), the *bajuband* or gold and stone-studded armlets, gold anklets and the *bichhiya* or gold toe-rings for the feet, and the *nath* or the stone-studded nose-ring.

- Most Maharashtrian Hindu brides get married in an emerald-green or topaz-yellow saree. These rich jewel colours woven with spun gold, find expression in traditional sarees like the Paithani, Narayanpeth, Induri, Chanderi, Puneri, Yeola and Irkali. This is the day for lavish jewellery and the bride wears gold, pearls and diamonds. A complete set of gold and pearl bangles makes music at her wrists. These are the pichodi, patli, toda, and bangdi which are interspersed with tinkling green glass bangles, the sign of marital prosperity and good luck. Her hair is styled and beautified with strings of fresh flowers called `gajra' and `veni'.

- All brides of South India wear 'Mangal-sutra' (their symbol of matrimony), offered by the husband to the bride and is the most precious ornament and it comes in from the ordinary to the most expensive studded with designs in gold and coloured stones.

- A traditional Muslim wedding dress for the groom consists of a 'churidar achkan', a 'kurta' embroidered with gold laces and a decorative 'fez'. The bride wears a white embroidered salwar kameez or colourful sari and exquisite pieces of jewellery, depending upon the financial status of the family.

More detailed descriptions of Indian wedding dresses can be found in an article :

" Indian Brides : Symbol of Pristine Beauty" by Mulk Raj Sidana, *India: Perspectives*, August 1998.

Wedding costumes in the Western style are not covered in this book. Readers would find some interesting details in Gallery of English Costume, *Weddings : Wedding costume, 1735-1970*, Canadian Museum of Civilization, Hull, 1977 ; Felger, Donna H, *Bridal Fashions : Victorian Era*, Canadian Museum of Civilization, Hull, 1986. Also, a cultural history of wedding in the Western society is traced in Charsley, S. R, *Wedding Cakes and Cultural History*, 1992.

4.4 Games and Testing the Groom

In some wedding ceremonies (e.g.,Bengali, Oriya, Maharashtrian, Rajasthani) games are arranged for fun by the bride's friends to test the strength and intelligence of the groom. He is conducted to the canopy for the marriage ceremony after he has passed these tests. For instance, the groom is required to be able to distinguish between two bowls containing curd and lime without tasting. Similarly, he may be asked to break a coconut without using the floor or split a big apple into two parts without using a knife. If he fails the test, he would have to pay the penalty with a piece of silver.

4.5 Regional Variations of Hindu Marriages

1. ORIYA WEDDING

- In Orissa, the worship of Krishna as Lord Jagannath is of supreme importance. Hence the first invitation card is sent to the Lord at the famous Jagannath temple at Puri.
- The Oriya Brahmins have their weddings only in the daytime, preferably mornings, whilst the non-Brahmin weddings are in the evening or night which is usual in most other communities.
- The engagement is called *Nirbandh*. The fathers of the bride and groom take an oath to wed their children to each other. In most communities, the engagement ceremony is held in the bride's home but in the Oriya community this is usually held in a temple.
- Wedding preparation begins with *Jairagodo Anukolo*, a ceremony which marks the stoking of the fire. The bride is blessed, and then anointed with turmeric and bathed, at a function known as *Mangono*. In the Oriya tradition, instead of going to a nearby river, water is collected from seven houses of relatives and friends for the ceremonial bath.
- Then the ritual called *Haatho Ghanti* follows where the couple walks around the fire seven times.
- Lastly the bride and groom are invited to the bride's house on the eighth day after the wedding, which is known as *Astha Mangala*.

2. TAMIL WEDDING

- In most cases Tamil marriages are conducted in public halls specially constructed for the purpose. As per the Hindu calendar, barring the months of Aashad, Bhadrapad, and Shunya, all other months are considered to be auspicious for marriage, as with most other Hindu weddings. An interesting episode in Tamil and Telegu weddings is 'Kashiyatra' (see below).

- *Panda Kaal Muhurtham* :
  The blessings of a protecting deity are solicited. The groom and his family are welcomed by the bride's family. It is a way of cementing the relationship between both the families. Then 'Vritham', prayer rituals to the family deity and *Naandi Shraartham* to honour ancestors and Brahmins follow.

- *Paalikali Thalippu* :
  Special clay pots are decorated with sandalwood paste and kumkum powder. Then *Lagna Pathirigai – Paddiputhu* follows, which means the bride and groom's families exchange sweets and invite each other to the wedding.

- *Jaanavaasam* :
  The groom arrives at the venue accompanied by friends and family, amidst fanfare, in a a big marriage procession , which is called 'Jaanavaasam'.

- *Nicchiyadharatham* :
  The priest performs Ganesh Puja with the bride's parents.

- *Mangala Snaanam* :
  The boy and the girl have an auspicious bath on the dawn of the wedding day.

- *Kashiyatra* :
  In Kashiyatra the groom pretends to be leaving for the pilgrimage to Kashi renouncing worldly life, when the bride's parents woo him to stay back and offer him gifts and their daughter's hands. Then the bride and groom exchange garlands thrice, handed to them by their respective maternal uncles.

- *Oonjal* :
  Then 'Oonjal' follows where the bride and groom are made to sit side by side on a swing. The swing is beautifully decorated with fresh flowers. This follows the Vaishnav tradition according to which the bride and groom are treated as the eternal consorts, Radha and Krishna.The groom is welcomed by the bride's father who washes his feet.

- *Kanya-Daanam* :

The groom and bride are symbolically united by the bride's father. The bride and groom go around the sacred fire seven times (Sapta-padi).

- *Sammandhi Mariyathai* :

An exchange of gifts between members of both families follows. All those present shower flower petals and 'akshata' on the couple in a ceremony called 'Paaladaanam'. Then the bride is formally received and welcomed into her new home and family ('Griha-pravesham').

3. TELEGU WEDDING

A Telugu marriage ceremony very much resembles a Tamil wedding. The following are the ceremonies performed :

- *Muhurtam* : Determining the auspicious time for the wedding.
- *Pendlikoothuru* : The bride and groom are anointed with oil and turmeric.
- *Snathakam* : The groom wears a silver thread.
- *Mangala Snaanam* : An auspicious bath is taken by both the bride and groom.
- *Kashi Yatra* : The boy pretends to be going for Kashi, renouncing worldly life. The parents of the bride persuade him to come back and offer various gifts.
- *Gauri Puja and Ganesh Puja* : Then the bride performs Gauri Puja. Ganesh Puja is also performed to carry out the function smoothly and without any obstacles.
- *Kanya-Daan* : where the girl is given away by her parents.
- *Jeelakarra- Bellamu* : A paste is applied to the bride and groom's hands.
- *Madhuparkam* : The boy and girl wear a white dhoti and sari.
- *Sumangalis* : The girl is accompanied by five pairs of married women.

- *Tying of the Mangal-sutra* : The necklaces symbolising marriage are tied by the bride and groom to each other.
- *Kanya- Daan Akshata* : The couple exchange garlands and are blessed by the elders.
- *Sapta-padi* : The couple takes seven steps together.
- *Sthaali-paakam* : The groom puts on silver toe rings on the bride's feet.

4. GUJRATI WEDDING

- *Kalash :*

A copper vessel with a coconut, and an idol of Lord Ganesh for the mandap mahuratis are considered essential.

- *Mandap Mahurat :*

The families of the bride and the groom perform this ceremony in their homes a few days before the wedding. The families pray to Lord Ganesh (the Hindu God, who is believed to remove all obstacles) and seek his divine blessing. The puja is performed by an acharya or priest in front of a sacred fire.

- *Graha Shanti:*

This is an important puja or prayer session and is conducted at the bride's home as well as the groom's. A mahurat or auspicious time is chosen for the puja after matching the horoscopes of the prospective bride and groom. This ritual springs from the belief that the stars and constellations exert influence on married life. Any disturbance in the stars can cause harm or clashes in the marital relationship and the lives of the couple. The purpose of the puja is to bring peace among the stars.

- *Jaan :*

This ritual involves the groom arriving at the house of the bride to seek the blessings of his mother-in-law. He must bow his head to his to-be mother-in-law. This gesture symbolises his humility. The groom's prospective mother-in-law blesses him and performs a small ritual to ward off the evil eye.

- *Kanya-daan :*

The bride is given away by both parents, sitting together, if both are alive. In some communities, only the father does this. They wash his feet as they believe that he is none other than the Hindu Lord, Vishnu, to whom they are handing over his rightful consort, the Goddess Laxmi in the form of their daughter. It may be noted that in some communities (in a traditional Bengali wedding, for instance, as mentioned later), the bride's mother and the groom's mother are not allowed to see the Kanya-daan ceremony. The reason for this could not be determined.

- *Hasta Milap:*

The groom's scarf or shawl is tied to the bride's saree. The priest chants mantras to invoke the blessings of Goddess Laxmi and Goddess Parvati for the saubhagyavrata or wife. The family and relatives present also come together to bless the couple and shower grains of rice and flower petals on them.

- *Pheras:*

The couple goes around the fire as the acharya chants mantras. The groom also recites mantras which express his heart's desire and seeks the loving support of his wife.

- *Sapta-padi:*

The couple must go around the holy fire seven times and take seven vows, as prescribed in the Rigveda.

- *Ghar nu Laxmi :*

The bride's first step into her new home is considered auspicious. She is the the Goddess Laxmi who will bring wealth and good fortune to her new home. In Gujrati there is a saying which means, "the house in which there is a happy bride Goddess Luxmi makes it her home". The bride is welcomed by her mother-in-law who performs a small ritual. She places a vessel, filled to the brim with rice, at the entrance of the house. The bride must knock the vessel down gently with her right foot, spilling some of the rice over. Using the left foot is considered inauspicious. Rice is a symbol of wealth.

5. PUNJABI WEDDING

People of the northern province of Punjab are a lively, vibrant, and a colourful race. In keeping with their racial character, the wedding ceremonies of the Punjabis are lively and colourful.

- *Sagan and Chunni Charana :*
  Both these rituals are performed close to the wedding date. Nowadays they are combined together for the sake of convenience.

  The ceremonies are usually conducted in a banquet or community hall. The priest performs a havan (a puja in front of a sacred fire). The father of the bride applies 'tilak' on the forehead of the groom. The bride is presented a red chunni (a traditional scarf) by the sister/sister-in-law of her future husband. She receives jewellery and gifts from her in-laws as part of the ceremony. Her mother-in-law feeds specially boiled rice and milk (Kheer) as part of the ritual. Finally, the prospective bride and groom exchange rings.

- *Mehndi Sang :*
  Days before the wedding, friends and close family members are invited and traditional wedding songs are sung at the bride's house. Sometimes professional dholwalis (female musicians who play the traditional drum) are invited for a special touch. Both sides exchange gifts and sweets. Hands and feet of the bride are decorated with mehndi. The henna is sent by the future mother-in-law.The ritual is marked by festivity. The girl friends and close female relatives of the bride-to-be sing and dance joyously on the occasion. After the application of henna, delicious snacks and meals are served to all present.

- *Ghara Ghardoli :*
  Bride-to-be stays at home in her old clothes for a couple of days before her wedding. She must sit in the vicinity of four lit oil lamps so that the glow from them is reflected on her face. All these measures are believed to contribute to a beautiful glowing look on her wedding day.

- *Vatna :*
  This is the Punjabi type ceremonial bath (Haldi ceremony). A sibling and the sibling's spouse usually fill a pitcher of water from a nearby temple and this water is added to the bath of the bride-to-be. Before her bath, *vatna* (a paste of powdered turmeric and mustard oil) is applied on her body by female relatives and friends. She is given a bath after this ritual and her old garments are given away to a poor person. Both, the ghara ghardoli and the vatna ceremonies are also performed for the groom at his house. Here the pitcher of water is brought for his bath by his *bhabi* (elder brother's wife).

- *Sehrabandi :*
  The groom's *sehra* or turban is blessed by his relatives. A young nephew or cousin also dons similar attire. He is called the *sarbala* (caretaker of the groom) and accompanies him on his mare or in his car. He is the Punjabi counterpart of the 'bestman' in the Western tradition. A puja is performed after the groom dons his wedding attire, as is the silver *mukut* or crown that goes on top of the turban. At the end of the ceremony, those present bless the groom and give him gifts or, more commonly, cash which is distributed among the poor. The groom's bhabi lines his eyes with *surma* (kohl). After this, the groom's sisters and cousins feed and decorate his mare. If the groom chooses to use a car for the occasion, then the car is decorated.

- *Milni :*
  The *milni* ceremony takes place when the groom's procession reaches the wedding venue. The groom and his relatives are welcomed with flower garlands by the bride's close relatives. The main aim of this ceremony is to help both sides get acquainted with each other. The girl's relatives give *shagun* to the groom's close relatives, beginning with his grandfather, father, uncles and brothers. The *shagun* usually consists of cash and is given away to the poor.

- *Muhurat* :

  When the muhurat or the auspicious time for the wedding ceremony approaches, the priest first performs a puja for the groom. The groom chants a few mantras. This is when the girl's young relatives steal the groom's shoes and hide them away to be returned after the ceremony for a reward. The reward – *kalecharis* – consists of gold for the bride's sisters and silver for her cousins.

- *Kanya-Daan* :

  The bride is given away by her father. This is followed by another ceremony – the pheras (rounds). The bride and groom go around the sacred fire with the bride's sari tied to the groom's clothing with the help of the red chunni used in the 'ghara ghardoli' ceremony. At the end of the ceremony, the newly-weds touch the feet of the groom's parents and the elders present to take their blessings. The bride changes into the clothes presented by her in-laws, while her relatives apply *tilak* on the groom's forehead.

- *Vidaai* :

  This ceremony marks the departure of the bride from her parental house and is called *vidai*. People throw *phulian* or puffed rice over her head. A beautifully decorated palanquin or car takes her to her new home. She is usually accompanied by her brother. Her relatives throw coins in the wake of this procession.

- *Pani Bharna* :

  The newly weds are welcomed in a ceremony called the *pani bharna*. The groom's mother performs the traditional aarti (puja) with a pitcher of water. The bride makes seven attempts to drink the water from the pitcher. The groom must allow her to succeed only at the seventh attempt.

- *Sarson ka Tel* :

  The bride must, with her right foot, kick a pot containing mustard oil that is put on the sides of the entrance door before she enters the house.

- *Phera Dalna* :

The newly weds visit the bride's parents a couple of days after the wedding. They are usually fetched by the bride's brother. This is comparable to the 'Dira Gaman' in a Bengali wedding. The bride's parents host a lunch to mark the occasion. They also give a lot of gifts to the newly weds.

6. MAHARASHTRIAN WEDDING

- *Muhurt* :

Soon after a match is made between a boy and a girl, the two families consult a priest and decide an auspicious day and time. The timing of the ceremony has to be precise so that the computation of the marriage rites after which the couple becomes husband and wife, coincides with the *muhurt* .

- *Devkarya* :

The days leading up to the wedding are filled with religious and social customs. As with any auspicious happening, divine blessings are sought before embarking on the festivities. The families of the bride and the groom are ceremonially invited by various friends and relatives to have a meal at a get-together known as *Kelvan.*

- *Haldi* :

The bride is anointed with turmeric paste by her female relatives as a rite of purification after which she is not supposed to leave her house till the wedding. The bridegroom is similarly anointed in his own home. Though not a Maharashtrian custom at all, these days, more and more brides are including decoration of their hands with mehendi. The bride's brother or relatives come to escort the groom and his family to the marriage hall, where they are ceremonially received by the bride's parents and family. Their feet are washed, they are garlanded and then led to the marriage pavilion or `mandap'. The mandap is always beautifully decorated with fresh flowers, usually marigolds and lilies or tube roses which suffuse the surroundings with their heavenly fragrance. The couple separately go through various ceremonies of welcome, offering and benediction with the respective families till the time of the muhurt draws near.

- *Antarpaat* :
  The first time the bride and groom stand face to face in the mandap is still a moment of separation as a decorated curtain called the `antarpaat' divides them, preventing them from seeing each other. Then the priest recites the `mangal-ashtaka' or the invitation to various gods to witness the marriage. Each of these recitations ends with `shubha mangala savdhan' which alerts everyone that the moment of the muhurt is approaching. Exactly at the muhurt, the antarpaat is removed and the bride and groom look at each other shyly to exchange garlands as the shehnai starts to play and the onlookers shower them with rice.

- *Kanya-Daan* :
  After this, the couple sits down to perform various ceremonies. The bride is ritually entrusted to the groom who promises to look after her in a ceremony called the `Kanya-Daan'. The husband and wife circle the holy fire which is the ultimate witness to their union. Then the husband guides his wife as she steps on seven little mounds of rice, promising her his friendship, love, and respect forever thereafter.

- *Manga-lsutra* and *Jodvi* :
  The bride is vested with the several symbols of marriage like the `mangal-sutra' on her neck and the `jodvi' on her toes. The couple performs the 'Laja-homa' with the bride's brothers, where sacrificial cereal and ghee are offered to the sacred fire.

With all these ceremonies completed, the couple then sits down to play various fun games much to the amusement of their family and friends. They are blessed by their elders, congratulated by their friends and presented with gifts to start their new life and make a home together.

7. MALAYALI WEDDING

The engagement ceremony in Kerala is called 'Kalyana Nischay'. The bride or the groom is not present.

Elders from both sides discuss the horoscopes of the boy and the girl after matching has already been done earlier. A 'Muhurtam' is agreed upon for the wedding in the presence of some community leaders and the astrologers. Sometimes, the alliance between the two families is written down and announced to all those invited. Two sides exchange gifts and sweets.

A traditional Malayali wedding is a relatively short and simple ceremony.   Most weddings are held at marriage halls. Usually, a portion of the hall is converted into a stage where the marriage ceremony takes place. As the auspicious hour dawns, the bride's mother lights a lamp at the venue of the wedding ceremony. This is a large ceremonial lamp---three to four feet high and made of brass. It is beautifully designed. In some Malayalam weddings, instead of fire, the bride and bridegroom circle this lamp (called 'Deepam').

Before leaving the house for the marriage venue, the groom pays respect to all the elders in his house. On the other hand, at the wedding hall an elaborate ceremony is arranged to welcome the groom. The bride arrives at the wedding place and a warm welcome is offered in a special, traditional manner and then she is made to sit next to the groom on the stage.

An important aspect of the Malayali wedding is 'Pudava Koda'---the groom offers to the bride a two- piece sari for her to wear thereafter on special occasions.

The groom ties the *Mangal-sutra* around the bride's neck which is blessed by the elders. The bride's father gives her hand to the groom (Kanya-Daan). An important ritual in a Malayali wedding consists of circling the holy fire or the ceremonial lamp three times (instead of the usual seven times).

Then the bride accompanies the groom to his house where she is welcomed in a ceremony called *Griha-pravesh*.

8. KANNADA WEDDING

A Kannada wedding is also relatively simple. A common feature of Kannada weddings is testing the abilities of the groom. Some of the ceremonies performed are quite common with the Tamil and Telegu weddings.

- The engagement ceremony is called *Nischay Tamulam.*
- *Nandi Puja* is performed to ensure that the wedding proceeds without any mishaps. Then the bride's and groom's families perform a havan at their respective homes before the groom goes to the bride's house.
- *Kashi Yatra :* Then the girl's father tries to prevent the groom from going on *Kashi Yatra* by offering gifts and his daughter's hand in marriage.
- *Kanya-Daan,* giving away of the girl to the groom follows.
- *Sapta-padi* : The bride follows the groom seven times around the holy fire and takes seven vows from the Rigveda.
- *Mangalashtam* is tied in the bride's neck and this completes the wedding.

9. MARWARI WEDDING

Marwaris were originally from the Marwar region of Rajasthan and traditionally a business community like the Parsis of Bombay. Since the Marwaris are of Hindu faith, their main wedding ceremony is very similar to that of other Hindu communities. Only some special customs are emphasized here.

- The engagement ceremony in Marwari community is known as *Sagaai.*
- Then the bride touches salt to ward off an evil eye, which is called *Namak Chhoona.*
- Another ritual called *Mangodi Todna* is performed where savouries are broken into pieces to avoid the evil.
- A day before the marriage, the groom accompanied by a group of women relatives visits the bride's house, the ritual is

called *Baan Chadana*. The ceremony takes place to ensure prosperity of the bride's and groom's houses.

- *Bhaat* is another ritual performed in the Marwari community. The mothers of the bride and the groom are honoured by their respective brothers. In a ritual called *Gor*, the girl receives her dowry from all her family members.

For the Marwaris, being a business community, giving and taking of gold jewellery and gold and silver coins (sikkas) is an important part of every ritual. Rich gifts display the lavishness with which the community has been associated.

- Then the actual wedding, comprising of the *saat pheras* and *Kanya-Daan,* takes place.
- The boy's sister ties a red thread around the girl's hair, it is called *Sirgutha*.
- *Anjala Bharna* is a ritual where the bride offers coins to her sister-in-law's husband. Then the girl is sent in a ceremonial way to her new house.
- After a few days the bride is invited to her parental home, which is known as *Pit Moda*.

10. RAJASTHANI WEDDING

Rajasthani or Rajput wedding is a very colourful ceremony and reflects a very old and colourful military tradition. The Rajputs (sons of kings) were a warrior class.

The official (engagement) ceremony takes place at the groom's house, not at the bride's house (contrary to the custom in other Hindu communities). Only the bride's father, brother and other close relatives attend this ceremony. This is a strictly all male affair. No ladies, not even the bride, accompany the men folk for the *tika*. The ceremony is so called because the bride's brother actually applies a *tilak* to the groom's forehead and makes the alliance or engagement official. A sword and other presents are offered to the groom.

- *Ganapati Sthapna*

The elephant-headed Lord Ganesh or Ganapati is worshipped and His blessings are requested for the event.

- *Pithi Dastoor*

  This ceremony follows which involves the bride/groom and continues until the day of the wedding. The actual ceremony consists of application of turmeric and sandal wood paste to the bride/ groom who cannot leave the house once the *pithi* starts.

  The pithi dastoor at the bride's house is an elaborate affair. The bride dresses in an orange poshak (Rajasthani dress) and is then brought under a silken canopy, which is held with the help of swords at the four corners by four ladies who must belong to the same clan as the bride.

  She is brought to the ladies' gathering, who then apply the paste to her. A similar ceremony takes place at the groom's place as well, although it is not that elaborate. Dholans (women singers with dholak) sing auspicious pre-wedding songs while the ceremony is in progress.

- *Mehfils*

  Mehfils or ceremonial gatherings are an integral part of every Rajasthani wedding. These are usually held in evenings, and they are segregated into the 'ladies mehfil' and the 'gents mehfil'.

  At the ladies' mehfil, all the womenfolk gather at a central place in an enclosed courtyard or hall. Dressed in dazzling dresses, they perform the *ghoomar* (a special dance done in a group). The bride at the mehfil is given an important position to sit and watch the proceedings.

- The *Mahira Dastoor*

  This is another important ceremony, common to both the bride and the groom's families. This ceremony is performed by the maternal uncle of the groom/bride, who, along with his wife and family, arrives with much fanfare, and is received by the bride/groom's mother with the traditional welcome. The uncle then distributes clothes, jewellery, and sweets to the entire family. The ceremony signifies that since at the time of a wedding there is considerable expenditure, it is the duty of the brother to help his sister at her child's wedding.

- *Janev*
Janev ceremony, where the sacred thread is given to the would- be groom on the eve of his becoming the house-holder. The janev is given only to men. The groom has to be dressed in saffron robes like an ascetic and perform a havan before wearing the thread.
The significance of saffron robes is that the groom now has two choices before him; either he renounces the world and becomes an ascetic, or he accepts the institution of marriage and its responsibilities.
After the havan is completed and the thread given, the groom has to make a mock attempt to run from the chains of marriage while the maternal uncle must catch him and convince his nephew into accepting marriage. This is similar to the Kashi Yatra described in the Tamil and Telegu weddings.

On the day of the actual wedding, or maybe a day prior to it, the *Palla Dastoor* is brought in by a few of the groom's relatives, accompanied by family retainers, to the bride's house. The palla dastoor consists of clothes, jewellery and gifts from the groom, which the bride has to wear during the wedding ceremony. This particular custom is typical of the Rajputs.

The actual wedding ceremony is similar to any other Hindu wedding. However, the bride must keep her face covered with a veil throughout the wedding ceremony.
After the bride reaches the groom's place *Griha-pravesh* takes place. The bride still wears the veil while the puja and other ceremonies take place. A few games are played between the bride and the groom. They are also common to other Hindu weddings. The day following the griha-pravesh, the *pagelagni* takes place. This is a ceremony where the bride, still in veil, is formally introduced to all the family members of the groom who bless her and give her gifts. The veil is then finally removed.

11. SINDHI WEDDING

Members of the Sindhi community (speaking the language Sindhi)
claim their origin to the Indus Valley Civilization. They were the
inhabitants of the valley of the river Sindhu (Indus).
They are of Hindu faith but over centuries have absorbed the rituals
and traditions of others including Sufism. Their wedding ceremony
follows the Vedic rites---some special customs commonly followed
by them only are mentioned below.

- *Kachi Misri*
  The engagement ceremony is called Kachi Misri. The family
  priests or some close relatives along with the boy and girl
  meet in a temple and exchange sweets (which must include
  crystallized sugar called Misri) as an indication to enter into a
  matrimonial alliance. If the marriage negotiations become
  acceptable to both parties, a formal engagement ceremony is
  arranged some time before the actual wedding at the girl's
  house and the girl's family sends gifts to the groom's house.
  This formal ceremony is called *Pakki Misri*.

- *Ukhiree-Muhiree*
  This ritual is performed by Ghot (bridegroom) and Kunwar
  (bride) separately at their residences. In this ritual in Ukhiree
  (Wooden pot) groom or bride thrashes Haldi (turmeric)
  pieces with Muhiree (wooden thick stick) into small pieces
  and ensures that crushed pieces do not come out. This
  indicates that when the groom or bride has to face difficulties
  he/she has to solve them in a sober way within the four walls
  of the house.

- *Ghadi-a-jo-Saath*
  After the wedding, the mother of the bride carries an earthen
  pot and goes out to the neighbourhood with family members
  and friends to the accompaniment of music and dancers. She

is escorted by her new son-in-law. After taking a round of the neighbourhood, she returns to the house and passes on the earthen pot to his new son-in-law. The significance of this ceremony is that the mother who brought up her daughter for many years now passes on the responsibility to the son-in-law.

- *Namak Chhoona*
  When the bride enters her new home, she touches a decorative bowl of salt. This signifies her fidelity to the new family of which she now becomes a part.

12. BENGALI WEDDING

The Bengali speaking people are now dispersed since the partition of India in 1947. The Bengalees residing in the state of West Bengal in India are mainly Hindus, while those residing in Bangladesh are mainly Muslims. But there are large numbers of Hindus still residing in Bangladesh and large numbers of Bengali speaking Muslims residing in India.

In a traditional Bengali Hindu wedding the usual Vedic rites are observed with some local customs and traditions. In a traditional Bengali Muslim wedding, Muslim rituals are observed. It seems that they have also absorbed some customs peculiar to Hindu tradition.

One of the unique features of a Bengali wedding ceremony is the blowing of a conch shell ('Shankha'), and sounding 'ulu ulu' occasionally. Also, decoration with the fragrant 'Rajanigandha' flowers is a unique feature of a Bengali wedding ceremony and celebration.

- It is common in a Bengali Hindu wedding to decorate the floors with 'alpona' and 'mangal kalash'. 'Alpona' consists of decorative motifs made with rice paste. Depicting fish signifying fertility and lotus symbolizing purity are an essential part of the decoration. 'Mangal Kalash' is a decorated earthen pitcher with mango leaves on top. The bride and the groom sit on special wooden seats made for this occasion that are artistically decorated with 'alpona'.

- At the wedding hall, the bride and groom sit on two wooden planks (*piris*). Decorated by a close friend or relative, these planks seat the bride and the groom during the wedding.
- According to a strange custom, in a traditional Bengali wedding, neither the bride's mother nor the groom's mother is allowed to watch the actual wedding ceremony. It is believed that it is inauspicious for them to watch it. The author has nowhere found a rational explanation for this strange custom.
- According to the Bengali custom, a wedding cannot take place in the Indian calendar months of Bhadra, Ashwin, Kartik, Poush and Chaitra.

The following are the usual ceremonies in a traditional Bengali wedding :

- *Paka-Dekha / Ashirvad* (Engagement)
  The engagement ceremony takes place in the bride's house. The groom's family pays a visit to the bride's house and blesses her in the presence of the invited relatives and friends. A piece of jewellery is presented to the bride symbolizing the alliance. This is conducted by a priest in the presence of an image of Satya Narayan.

- *Gaye Halud* (Ceremonial bath)
  The groom's family sends turmeric, oil, clothes, cosmetics, fish and sweets to the bride's house for the ceremonial bath and the bride's family reciprocates.

- *Dodhi Mangal*
  On the wedding day, the bride's wedding day starts very early before the sunrise, with *dodhi mangal* ceremony. Seven married

women accompany the bride to a nearby pond where they invoke the Goddess Ganga to the wedding and use a pitcher of the pond water to bathe the bride. After this, she is offered some curd and this is the only foodstuff she is allowed to eat until the wedding ceremony is completed.

- *Varan* (ceremonial welcoming of the groom by bride's mother and others)

- *Mala Badal* (Exchanging garlands) and *Shubha Dristi* (Auspicious meeting of eyes)
  The bride and the groom exchange garlands to signify their mutual acceptance and union. The bride and the groom see one another under a canopy.

- *Kanya-Daan* (Bestowal of bride)
  The bride's father or some elderly person designated by the family offers the girl to the groom in marriage.

- *Granthi-bandhan* (Tying the ends of the clothes of the couple)

- *Kushandika* (Fire ritual)

- *Sapta-padi* (Seven steps or vows)

- *Phool Sajja*
  This is an in-house honeymoon after the wedding at the groom's house.

- *Bashi Biye*
  The morning after wedding, the groom adorns the forehead of his bride with vermillion. He does this by looking into a mirror.

- *Bodhu Baran :* Welcoming the new bride

- *Bou Bhat* (Wedding Reception)

In the wedding reception, or prior to this, the newly wed bride serves food to the family members and close relatives with her own hands. She receives a lot of gifts from them as a token of their appreciation and good wishes.

- *Dira Gaman* (Second visit)

A ceremony is conducted when the newly-weds visit the bride's house for the first time a few days after the wedding. The thread that was tied by the priest on the bride's wrist during the wedding rituals is cut during this ritual. Conch shells are blown to the accompaniment of the sounds of 'ulu ulu' to mark the auspicious moment.

In North America

In North America at least it has become a popular practice to sing one of the famous songs of the celebrated Indian Nobel Laureate, Rabindranath Tagore. I have witnessed this in several Bengali weddings in USA and Canada. The English translation of this song is reproduced below :

On this day of romantic union
The one who is the true witness
I salute Him---I salute Him again and again.
The one who is omniscient and constant
Companion in prosperity and in distress
In good times and bad---
I salute Him--- I salute Him again and again.

In the dark night whose glances are in the stars
Whose glances are beyond life and death
Whose glances are in the burning flame of the sun
Lord of the heart of the living---
I salute Him--- I salute Him again and again.

All the deeds of this life
All the duties of this material world
Bestow onto His feet
The one who is the witness of this universe
And Lord of the heart---
I salute Him--- I salute Him again and again.
(Translated by Arun S. Roy)

13. BRAHMO SAMAJ WEDDING

Background

- The Brahma / Brahmo Samaj, an important sect of Hinduism, emerged in Bengal and was founded by Raja Ram Mohan Roy in 1828. It rejected idol worship and the worship of multiple gods and goddesses of the traditional Hindu faith.
- Raja Ram Mohan Roy was much influenced by western thought, especially Christianity. The followers of Brahmo Samaj believe in formless ('Nirakar') God. They are worshippers of Hindu God, Brahma (the supreme creator). The followers of Brahmo Samaj attach less significance to the rituals. They embraced several liberal ideas of the West and propagated education among women and discouraged early marriages of girls.
- Some notable followers and leaders of the Brahmo Samaj Movement in Bengal were Keshab Chandra Sen, Debendra Nath Tagore, Rabindra Nath Tagore, and Shib Nath Shastry.
- The major factor that contributed to the emergence of the Brahmo Samaj was that the social system in the Hindu community became stagnant and placed too much emphasis on traditional rituals. The growth in the Brahmo Samaj movement was halted due to numerous social reforms and progressive changes in the practice of the Hindu faith.

Wedding Ceremony

Brahmo Samaj wedding ceremonies are relatively simple and less ritualistic.

In a Brahmo Samaj wedding, the bride and the groom, as adults, declare in an open house that each is willing to accept the other as a partner for life. Thus a Brahmo Samaj wedding has no tradition of "giving away" the daughter by her parents.

The Brahmo Samaj priest ('Acharya') presides over the wedding ceremony. The priest does not have to be a male, neither does he have to be a Brahmin, unlike in a traditional Hindu ceremony. Any knowledgeable respectable person of the community can act as the Acharya.

- There is no 'Sapta-padi' nor is there circling the fire by the couple.
- Officially taking the consent of the bride and the bridegroom ('sammati' and 'anumati') in front of the congregation is an essential part of the ceremony.
- The Acharya recites prayers from the Upanishads [MN-9]. It is common to recite the following verses from the Upanishad :

> *Asato ma sadgamah*
> *Tamaso ma jyotirgamah*
> *Mrityurma amritam gamah*

> (Oh Lord Brahma, the creator, the supernatural)
> Lead us from falsehood to truth.
> Lead us from darkness to light.
> Lead us from death to immortality.

In addition, the Acharya usually composes an appropriate personal prayer and benediction for the couple and reads it out to the assembly. Prayers are complemented by singing of musical compositions based on the Upanishad.

- The marriage is solemnised by tying the right hands of the bride and the groom with flower garlands. Exchanging rings as in Christian wedding is also common.
- A book of marriage is then signed by the bridegroom, bride and some witnesses, resembling a simple type Christian wedding in modern times.

14. ARYA SAMAJ WEDDING

Background

The Arya Samaj was founded in 1875 by Swami Dayanad of Punjab. Like Raja Mohan Roy of Bengal, he was a social reformer. But instead of propagating the liberal ideas of the West he devoted his life to propagating the Vedic religion. He advocated unity of human race and aimed at reforming the Hindu religion and society by making it more egalitarian and less ritualistic. For this reason, the wedding ceremony as practiced by members of the Arya Samaj is claimed to be relatively simple and less ritualistic. The followers of the Arya Samaj in their wedding ceremony place a greater emphasis on the inner meaning of marriage and less on the rituals. The Arya Samaj also believes that the institution of marriage is a code prescribed in the Vedas. To quote a verse which is recited during the Lajahoma:

Sarasvati predamava subhage vajinivati.
Yantva vishvasya bhutasya prajayama
syagrtah Yasyam bhutam samabhavat
yasyam vishvamidam jagat. Tamadya
gatham gasyami ya strinam yashah.
(Paraskar, 1, 2).

"O bride! You are the symbol of culture, source of all round pleasure and happiness and the mistress of grain and wealth. Protect and strengthen this conjugal affinity. You represent the Prakriti, the material cause of this universe..."

Here the couple is representative of Prakriti and Purusha--the couple responsible for the creation of the universe. The establishment of the institution of marriage is thus believed to be simultaneous with the emergence of mankind on earth and the procedure of marriage is likened to the story of creation. Almost every human being, according to the Vedas, has the obligation to discharge certain debts. One of these is known as Pitri Rina or the Parental debt which is cleared by maintaining the continuity of generation. Thus reproduction is considered to be the critical aspect in marriage. As man has the obligation to propagate his species, a matrimonial affinity becomes essential.

As the Arya Samaj was a reaction against superstitions, horoscopes are avoided and any day or time of mutual convenience is regarded as acceptable for the ceremony.

Wedding Ceremony

Since the Arya Samajists believe in the Vedic rites, the ceremony basically follows a typical Hindu ceremony but there are no local customs as are observed in various regions. Understanding the marriage vows that are taken and their significance is emphasized.

The wedding is conducted according to Arya Marriage Validation Act XIX of 1937 and is solemnized according to Vedic rites. In these weddings, the pooja is not performed to any specific deity because the Samaj doesn't believe in idol worship. Fire and the other elements of Nature are the only witnesses to the ceremony.

The ceremony consists of the following, most of which are a part of the traditional Hindu ceremony . Most of these have been discussed in detail in the Hindu wedding ceremony :

- 'Madhuparka' (Sweet holy water given to the groom)
- 'Pratigya Mantra' and 'Panigrahan'(The husband makes marital vows holding his wife's hands. (see below)

- 'Homa' (sacrificial fire)
- 'Parikrama' (The couple take four rounds of the fire one for each four ashrams in the Vedic age)
- 'Sapta-padi' (Seven steps and marital vows by the couple)
- 'Lajahoma' (offering puffed rice to fire)
- 'Shilarohan' (The bride places her foot on a stone slab as part of the Lajahoma and the bridegroom says" ascend this stone and be firm like a rock..."
- 'Hriday Sparshan' (Symbolic event in which the bride and the groom reach out to each other to touch one another's hearts)
- 'Sindoor Daan' (A common Indian tradition of applying of Sindoor on the wife's hair parting by her husband)
- 'Dhruv Darshan' (As the couple is ready to begin their new life they are shown the dhruv or the pole star to celebrate marital bliss)
- 'Surya-namaskar' (A prayer to the Sun for good health and prosperity, in the morning following the wedding).

Madhuparka

As the groom arrives at the bride's home he is given water to drink and to wash his feet and face. He is then given madhuparka or a mixture of honey and curd. At the time he chants a hymn which reads:

"Sweet are the breaths of winds.
Sweet is the flow of rivers.
Let herbs be full of sweetness for us.
Night is sweet and so is the dawn.
Sweet is earthly sand.
Let vegetable kingdom be sweet for us and sweet be the sun.
Let cows give us sweet milk."

Pratigya Mantra

Vows are taken by the groom holding the hands of the bride. The following is the vow as translated in English :

I, the bridegroom hold your hand into mine for prosperity of household life. May you attain old age with pleasure along with me as your husband. God, who is the master of all prosperity, the administrator of justice, the creator of the universe and all-subsisting; and the enlightened persons here are giving you to me for the fulfillment of household life's attainments and obligations.

15. ASSAMESE WEDDING

The traditional Assamese Hindu wedding follows the usual Hindu wedding ceremonies---'Kanya-Daan', fire ritual, 'sapta-padi' and 'sindurdaan'.
But an Assamese wedding is spread over a period of three days. The first day is called 'juran diya'. If the families do not live too far from one another, the groom's family visits the bride's family and gives some gifts to bride and her mother.
The second day is called 'adhivasa'. The bride, groom and their mothers observe a fast on this day and at the end of the day make offerings to god praying for a happy married life for the would-be couple.
The third day is the wedding day. A ceremony called 'daiyan diya' is observed in the morning. Curd (yogurt) is sent to bride's house from the groom's house and the bride takes half of the curd and returns the other half to the groom. Both bride and groom are then given the ceremonial bath with oil turmeric and curd.
On the wedding day as the groom arrives, he is welcomed by his mother-in-law at the gate of the bride's house and the bride's younger sister washes his feet. She in return gets a cash gift from the groom. He is then led to the wedding hall and the bride joins him.
The maternal uncles of the bride and of the groom tie the end of the bride's sari to that of the groom's shawl. In the fire ceremony mango stems are offered as an essential offering in an Assamese wedding.
The kanya-daan or offering of the bride to groom's family is done by

the father of the bride. At the conclusion of the wedding, the bride and groom are asked to exchange betel leaves, specially made with fragrant spices for the occasion.

After the wedding the couple is made to play a game in which a ring is put into a vessel containing rice and the couple has to put their hands in and search for the ring. It is said that whoever finds the ring first wins and will dominate in the household life.

16. KASHMIRI WEDDING

Kashmiri wedding is a very colorful ceremony reflecting the beautiful and colorful landscape of the land of Jammu and Kashmir. One part of Kashmir in India, the other part is in Pakistan. In the State of Jammu and Kashmir, there are large numbers of Hindus, but the majority of the inhabitants are Muslim.

Kashmiri Hindu Wedding

Most of the customs and ceremonies that are observed in a Kashmiri Hindu wedding ceremony are similar to those in other parts of India, but there are some special features as well, as described below.

* *Vanna* (Formal Engagement)

Once the two families agree to the alliance, a formal commitment (or *vanna*) ceremony takes place in the form of *kasamdry*. The ceremony takes place in the bride's house. In olden days it was held in a temple. The girl's family invites the boy's family. They exchange flowers as a sign of celebration of the formalisation of the alliance. The eldest aunt of the girl prepares 'var' (a special rice pudding) which is distributed among the the guests, neighbour and relatives.

* *Livun* (House Cleaning)

A few days before the wedding, an interesting ritual called Livun is observed in both the bride and groom's houses. Livun means ceremonially cleaning the house to drive away evil spirits. Women family friends, relatives, and neighbours help in this. This is more common and is a bigger event in villages than in the urban society. At the end of the day, all the participants in Livun are treated with a feast. Sometimes a Livun ceremony is combined with *wanwan* or ladies sangeet in which bride's friends and relatives sing traditional Kashmiri wedding songs (*vachun*).

- *Sanzvaru*

The boy's family sends *sanzvaru* for the bride. This contains cosmetics, a small mirror, *sindoor*, a shawl and also special paan or betel leaf encased in silver and gold warq or foil. The bride dresses for the wedding using these cosmetics.

- *Diugun*

Diugun takes place on the morning of the wedding day separately in the houses of the bride and the groom. The elders in the respective families apply a paste of curd, gram flour *(besan)* and saffron to the bride's and groom's heads. Then the bride and the groom take a bath (in their respective houses).

Then there is a *pooja* separately in the houses of the bride and the groom . After this *puja*, the bride, the groom and their respective parents observe a fast till the wedding is over. The parents of the bride give her jewellery, clothes, household items, etc. An essential item of the jewellery is the *dijaru*, an ear ornament, which is the symbolic ornament of a married Kashmiri woman as a 'sakha' (as a conch shell bangle is in a Bengali marriage, or a 'mangal-sutra' is among the South Indians).

- *Jaiphal*

As the groom's party arrives for the wedding ceremony, the fathers of the bride and the groom exchange *jaiphal* or nutmeg. It is believed that the root of nutmeg is indestructible. It binds the two families in an eternal relationship.

Kashmiri Muslim Wedding

A Muslim wedding traditionally follows the usual Muslim customs. But there are some special features.

- *Thap*

'Thap' literally means to catch somebody and in this ceremony the boy and the girl engage each other for a marriage. The meeting of the boy and the girl is often arranged outside the home, in public places such as a mosque or a public park (although it is not uncommon these days to meet in a house also).

The main reason for meeting outside is that if the boy does not approve of the girl, the two can separate easily without any obligation.

When the couple accepts each other, the Thap is followed by an engagement ceremony. Jewellery is often given to the bride by the groom's family, and sometimes rings and flowers are exchanged. After the exchange of rings and flowers the two families return to their respective homes.

- *Muchravum*

On the wedding day, this function is organised at the girl's place and is called 'Muchravum'. On this day the girl ties small plaits to her hair, which are later unbraided by all the married ladies of the family. The ladies unbraid the plaits and apply oil to the bride's hair. The function is accompanied by a good amount of fun and teasing and winds up with everyone showering their choicest blessings on the bride.

- Nikah Ceremony

The girl applies mehendi on her palms and legs. The girl's family presents the boy's family members with 'shatush' shawls (made from the hide of the shatush deer). On this day the bride is given a bath (*ghusul*) by her mother and aunts and then she is dressed in the traditional Kashmiri dress.

The groom wears a special turban called 'karakuli topi' when he enters the bride's house. At the wedding ceremony the 'nikaah' is read by the 'maulvi' (priest). The amount of the meher is fixed at this time. Meher is a sum of money, which the husband has to give his wife during her lifetime. In case there is a divorce the amount has to be given as part of the divorce settlement.

Chapter 5

Muslim Marriage

5.1 Background and Founding of Islam

- The religion of Islam was founded by Muhammed (570-632 C.E.) in Arabia. Muhammed was born in a poor family and became an orphan at an early age. He was brought up by his uncle. Muhammed was illiterate and worked as a caravan driver for a wealthy widow (Khadija) whom he later married.

- The Arabian peninsula was in a state of constant religious feuds and people worhipped a multitude of gods and idols. Idolatry was the dominant form of worship among the Jews, and Zoroastrians as well as among many tribal groups. Paganism was the common way of life. Islam developed and spread as a reaction to idolatry and Paganism.

- Muhammed received revelations from an angel, a messenger of God, whom he identified as Gabriel. These divine messages, when written, became the scriptures of Islam, the Koran (meaning ("recitation")). *Islam* in the Arabic language literally means submission.

- The Koran is believed by faithful Muslims to be God's last word to humanity. The Koran is organized into 114 chapters, called *surahs*. These are believed to be the exact words of Allah from the Prophet from the time of the first revelation to the end of Muhammed's life. The sayings, judgements, and other messages from his life had been compiled by his followers after the Prophet's death and these are known as *Hadith*.

- Unlike Hindu scriptures (which are many), the Koran does not prescribe any special passages to be recited for solemnising a Muslim wedding.

Instead of footnotes, some details are placed at the end of the
book under the title " Miscellaneous Notes" (MN---numbered).

5.2 Essentials of Islamic Faith

Islam is opposed to any form of idolatry.
The "Five Pillars of Islamic Faith" are
- Belief in one God, Allah
- Reciting prayers five times a day
- Giving charity and doing charitable work
- Periodic fasting
- Once in a lifetime at least one pilgrimage to Mecca

Shias and Sunnis
There are two sects among the Muslims---Shias and Sunnis. As
discussed later, their marriage customs are slightly different. The
essential difference between the two sects is that the Sunnis adhere to
the orthodox tradition and acknowledge the first four Caliphs as the
rightful successors of Muhammed. Shias, on the other hand, believe
that the first three Caliphs were usurpers. The fourth Caliph (Ali),
Muhammed's son-in-law, and the Imams are the only rightful
successors of Muhammed. Sunnis are in the majority (about 90%)
and Shias are a minority.

5.3 Evolution of Marriage in Islam

A few words might be useful in understanding the institution of
Muslim marriage by putting it in the historical context.
In pre-Islamic Arabia, there were four kinds of marriage prevalent
among the nomads of Arabia :
- Marriage by capture
- Marriage by friendship
- Marriage by contract
- Temporary marriage

Marriage by capture meant that women and wealth were captured through tribal warfares. Women were considered as valuable for reproduction and tribes attacked their enemies to capture as many as possible.

In marriage by friendship, the male approached the woman and offered her his friendship. The Arabic word for this was *sadiqa*. There were no witnesses, and possibly no formal wedding ceremony. The man gave a gift reflecting the woman's value.

In marriage by contract, the prospective husband drew up a contract with the girl's father to buy his future wife from him. On delivering the purchase price (called *Mahr*) , the bride was delivered. Prophet Muhammed prescribed marriage by contract as the legal marriage in the Koran.

In temporay marriage (*muta* marriage) a man paid a woman for a specified length of time for cohabitation. It was terminable at the will of either party. The Muslim sect known as *Sunnis* (orthodox sect) believe this to be unlawful. *Shias* (a second Muslim sect), on the other hand, believe that temporary marriage was sanctioned by Koran as long as the Mahr is paid and they still continue to practice this.

5.4 Marriage Customs in Islam

The Koran states that it is the religious duty of all to get married. It is recommended that all girls should be married by the father or the guardian before they reach the age of puberty. In traditional Muslim families, it is usually the parents or other guardians who take an active part to arrange marriages of their sons and daughters. With the spread of education, and intermixing of boys and girls, parents are beginning to accept the choice of their children in a large measure in matrimony. The average age at marriage in the urban Muslim communities is no different from that in other religious communities. The Arabic word for a pair or a mate is *zawj*, which is a term used for marriage (*al-zawaj*). Alternatively the term *nikah*, is also used and refers to sexual union. This union is formalized through a marriage contract. This contract is between the two parties, usually under the initiative of fathers or guardians.

The marriage must be publicly proclaimed, and it is recommended that it is held in a public place.

- Mutual Consent

Islam prohibits marriage by force or coercion and as such consent of both the bride and bridegroom is an essential element of the matrimonial contract (*Hadith*, Bukhari: 67: 42 & 43). The mutual consent of the bride and bridegroom is verified in the presence of eligible witnesses. The wedding ceremony, especially the mutual consent part, must be witnessed by witnesses from both parties.

- Bride Price (Mahr)

In a Muslim marriage, bride price or groom-dowry (*mahr*) is an essential component of the matrimonial contract. This is comparable to and is very similar to what is found in a Jewish marriage. In a traditional Muslim wedding, *Mohar* (also known as *mahr*) is the dowry given by the groom to the bride.
No specific amount is specified as the bride price in the Koran. It all depends upon the husband's wealth and bride's status. As the Koran (2: 236) states " ...the wealthy according to his means, and the poor according to his means."
The bride price remains hers even in the event of a divorce and she can retain half of it if the marriage is dissolved before consummation. As the Koran says, "if ye divorce them before ye have touched them and ye have appointed them a portion, then pay the half of that which ye appointed..."
(Koran 2 : 237)

- Kabin Nama

The amount of Mahr is specified and is written in the form of a legal document or contract (*Kabin Nama*), usually prepared by lawyers of the two sides. The Kabin Nama states whether any amount is paid fully at the time of marriage or it is paid partially, the remainder to be paid later during the married life. Kabin Nama also contains some personal information relating to the bride and groom, and names and addresses of the witnesses signing the document. The Kabin Nama is similar to *Khetuba* that is customarily prepared in Jewish marriages.

- Non-Muslim Partner

Islam puts some restrictions on Muslims marrying non-Muslims. A Muslim girl is prohibited to marry a non-Muslim husband. Koran (2 : 21) states that " And do not give (a Muslim woman) to idolators until they have accepted Islam , and certainly a believing slave is better than an idolator even though he should please you."
A Muslim man, however, is allowed to marry a woman who is not an atheist. Koran (5:5) states " And the chaste from among the believing women and the chaste from among those who have been given the book before you (are lawful for you) when you have given them their marriage portion taking them in marriage." The phrase "those who have been given the book before you" refers to Jews and Christians.

- Polygamy

Islam permits upto a maximum of four wives at one time. The Koran qualifies this, however, by stating that provided the husband can treat all the wives equitably (Koran, 4:3). The English translation is the following :

> "… marry women of your choice, two, three, or four ;
> but if you fear you shall not be able
> to deal justly (with them), then only one ."
> (English translation, *The Noble Quran in the English Language by* Al-Hilali and M.M. Khan)

It is possible that when tribal feuds and civil wars took heavy tolls of lives of men, and women outnumbered men of marriageable age, it was important to allow and probably encourage polygamy.

Some Islamic scholars infer from the qualifying condition above that since treating all wives justly (equally) is virtually impossible, the intent of Islam is in fact monogamy and not to encourage polygamy.

- Widow Remarriage

Islam permits widow marriage. Prophet himself married widows. As the plight of widows must have been deplorable in olden days, it was necessary to encourage widow remarriage---something which the patriarchal Hindu society vehemently denied to the widows in India for centuries. The injustice and indignity that the widows in a Hindu society were made to suffer for a long time were barbaric and cruel. (see discussion elsewhere in this book).

- Prohibited Marital Relationship

Certain women are totally forbidden for marriage if the relationship is: mother, daughter, sister, paternal aunt, maternal aunt, brother's daughter, sister's daughter, mother-in-laws, daughter-in-law, step-mother, step-daughter, foster mother, foster sister (Koran : 4:23). Among Muslims, as in South India marriage between cousins is encouraged, both cross-cousins (the children of a brother and sister) and parallel cousins (the children of two same-sex siblings).

- Age at marriage

No minimum age is specified for marriage partners in the Koran. Thus theoretically, child marriages may be considered as legal under Islam. For this ambiguity some Muslim countries such as Turkey have specified the minimum age for marriage.

5.5 Muslim Wedding Ceremony

- Developing as it did as a reaction against idolatry, animism, and paganism, a marriage ceremony in the Muslim community is austere and rather simple. This is in contrast with other religions including Jewish, and Christian marriages, not to talk of a Hindu marriage.

- Also, in contrast with other religious communities, the ceremonies are not very different geographically. A Muslim marriage in a Middle Eastern country would be very similar to the one in Africa.

  However, some local Hindu customs have inadvertently crept into the Muslim marriage ceremony in India and have remained a part of the same. For instance, fixing of an auspicious date for a wedding ceremony is often done by an astrologer, a typical Hindu custom. In wedding ceremonies in the Bengali Muslim community, prior to wedding both the bride and bridegroom are bathed in water specially prepared with turmeric paste. This is also a traditional Hindu custom (see discussion elsewhere in this book) .

- After the party of the bridegroom arrives at the bride's home, tastefully decorated for the special occasion, it is received by the bride's family. Often arrangements are made for a party of musicians to play music on the occasion. A mullah who performs the ceremony approaches the bride and bridegroom separately in the presence of witnesses to ascertain whether the bride and the bridegroom have their consent to the marriage. Traditionally, this is done in separate congregations of the bride and bridegroom. They are asked this question, not once but three times. A marriage contract like a legal document is signed by the couple and the witnesses.

Marriage Sermons

The marriage contract is sanctified by sermons. The sermon (*Khutbah*) includes recitation from the Koran as well as those words recommended by Prophet Muhammad. A part of the sermon reads:

"O humanity,
be reverent toward your Lord
who created you from one soul
and created its mate from it,
and these two
disseminated many men and women.
Be reverent toward God
by whom you ask of each other,
and be reverent toward relationships,
for God is watching over you". (Koran, 1-10)

In addition to the foregoing verse, the priest may select other verses from the Koran to be recited for the benefit of the couple and the congregation.

This completes the ceremony and they are declared husband and wife.

While the rituals of wedding ceremony mostly depend upon local customs, kissing in public is not seen during a Muslim wedding.

One of the widely practiced rituals is to have the bride and the groom seated together side by side with a mirror placed in front of them. Having been dressed up for the wedding, they are then given the chance to look in the mirror, as if they are seeing each other for the first time. The significance of using a mirror for exchanging glances at one another on this occasion is rooted in an ancient Muslim tradition. This is meant to ward off the evil spirit having a spell on the bride or the groom. It is believed that an evil spirit or ghost does not have an image in a mirror.

Well-wishers give gifts on this occasion. A feast is recommended and normally takes place when the bride comes to the husband's house.

Islam and Divorce

In Islam, there are three major types of divorce :

Mubaraat : This is a divorce by mutual agreement where both parties desire a divorce.

Khul : This form of divorce is at the instance of the wife upon agreeing to give a consideration to the husband for releasing her from the marriage tie.

Talaq : This is a repudiation of the marriage by the husband by the pronouncement of 'talaq'. When a husband utters the word talaq three times, the divorce becomes legal.

It is commonly but mistakenly believed that this pronouncement (*Talaq hasan*) can be done all at once. It is not permissible to pronounce the three repudiations all at once time. Talaq hasan requires three successive pronouncements of divorce to be made during three consecutive periods of purity (*tuhur*).

After divorce the woman should wait three monthly cycles during which her husband remains responsible for the welfare and maintenance. He is not permitted to drive her out of the house during this period but she may leave it if she wishes.

The main purpose of this waiting period is to ascertain whether the divorced wife is expecting a child. Its second use is as a cooling-off period during which the relatives and other members of the family or of the community may try to help towards a reconciliation and better understanding between the partners. The Koran says:

"And if you fear a breach between the two, then appoint a judge from his people and a judge from her people; if they both desire agreement, Allah will effect harmony between them, surely Allah is Knowing, Aware." (4:35).

However, even after reconciliation of two times, if the husband declares divorce for a third time, the divorce becomes irrevocable. For him to re-establish his matrimony to the wife, she must be married to another person, formally divorced by him, and only then she has to be remarried to the former husband.

Interpreters of Koran and Hadith believe that divorce should be resorted to only as a last resort and in cases of irreconciliable differences. The Prophet said: "Of all the things Allah has permitted, the one He most dislikes is divorce". If divorce becomes inevitable, the Koran prescribes for men to treat them well : "Once you divorce women and they have reached the end of their waiting period, then either retain them in all decency or part from them in decency. Do not retain them unjustly so that you exceed the limit; anyone who does that merely hurts himself" (2:231).

Dissolution of marriage in Muslim society in India takes place through Court under the Dissolution of Muslim Marriage Act of 1939. The Act specifies nine grounds for dissolution of marriage and include impotency and insanity of the husband etc. For details about the status of Muslim women in India, see Shaheeda Lateef, *Muslim Women in India*, Zed Books, London, 1990.

5.6 Muslim Marriages Outside India

In countries other than India, in the Muslim communities, there are hardly any differences in the sacramental part of the ceremony whether it is marriage in a Shia or a Sunni community. Some of the marriage customs differ, however. These customs vary widely in the traditional tribal communities , which is beyond the scope of this book. The following observations can be made with regard to the mainstream Muslim communities.

- In Turkey, one of the most liberal Muslim countries, the right of the guardian who could enter into a marriage contract has been rescinded.
  The minimum age for marriage has been established and all marriages solemnized by the clergy must be registered for approval.
- In Saudi Arabia, the country of birth of the Prophet , arranged marriages are more common and the Western style courtships and dating are rare. The Western type free mixing of the sexes is socially unacceptable. There is a great deal of segregation between males and females and social interactions are not normally tolerated. Virginity and chastity of women are considered to be very important for the marital relationship. A family tolerating the loss of virginity by a woman before marriage may be socially ostracized.
- If an adult man takes fancy for a young woman, he must approach a friend to make a proposal to the woman's family. They are normally allowed to meet in the presence of other adults. Elders of the two families negotiate and compare the

attributes of the bride and bridegroom and family backgrounds before paving the way to a matrimonial alliance.

- The ideal marriage in some Muslim countries is between the first cousins. In many traditional Muslim families, words of matrimony are exchanged even before the girl reaches the age of puberty. One reason for this kind of preferred marriage custom is that ancestral landed and other property remains within the extended family. Secondly, both the bride and the groom families are well known to one another. The two parties would be known to be of good moral character. Thirdly, any marital disputes at a later stage can sometimes be resolved amicably within the family.

- The bride-price or the groom-dowry ('mahr') is often quite heavy. Adult men that are poor and are unable to save enough to pay the groom-dowry remain unmarried. There are foundations in some countries (more commonly found in Saudi Arabia) created with donations from the wealthy people that give grants to needy bachelors that are willing to marry. One condition is that the local Imam must certify that the recipient agrees to be a devout Muslim and will do prayers according to the Koran.

- Upto a maximum of four wives are permitted but Muslim societies are trending towards monogamy.

In some African countries polygamy is still very common especially in wealthy and prosperous families. The wives are classified as 'inside wives' (main) and 'outside wives' (subsidiary). The subsidiary wives do not live in the household but the husband is legally responsible for their maintenance and protection.

5.7 Women In Islam

In recent years with the human rights movement and the emergence of gender issues, there is an attempt to reassess the status of women in Islam by scholars in general and feminists in particular. A variety of questions have been raised.

- Did the Koran place women on equal footing with men as has often been claimed ?
- Has the interpretation of the Islamic law been fair to the Muslim women ?
- Has the status of Muslim women changed with the changes in social and economic conditions in the contemporary world ?
- Should the interpretation of the Koranic law change in response to changes in the social and economic structure ?
- Has the status of Muslim women kept pace with changes in the rights and privileges accorded to women in other religions?

These are extremely complex issues and are highly controversial. These are also likely to evoke a great deal of religious sentiments and emotions. Very recently, a Canadian journalist and author, Irshad Manji, has provided a comprehensive survey of feminist issues relating to Islam (see her recent book, *The Trouble With Islam*, Random House, 2003)

Only some views of the recognized scholars in the field are quoted below without any attempt to draw definite conclusions.

Islam a Definite Improvement

There is ample evidence to suggest that when a comparison is made between the status of women in the pre-Islamic period with that in the Islamic period in the Arab world , there was a definite improvement. Islam improved the status of women :

(i)	by restricting polygamy to four wives concurrently,
(ii)	by assigning a share of inheritance to women ,
(iii)	by declaring Mahr as a gift to the bride ,
(iv)	by reorienting the Arab law of marriage and divorce in favour of women , and
(v)	by condemning female infanticide.

These were indeed revolutionary with the founding of Islam.

Pre-Islamic Arab World

- During the Pre-Islamic period, the Arab countries were characterized by unstable marriage relationships, polygamy, lack of fidelity and chastity among women as well as men, prevalence of slavery, and women generally not having rights to property. Although historical records are limited, available folklores and literary themes confirm many of these characteristics of the Pre-Islamic Arab world. When the Koranic commandments and prescriptions are placed against this socio-religious background, their significance and rationale become much clearer.

- Women captured in the warfare were either kept as mistresses in the harem or given the status of a married wife. In addition, the father or the kin of an unmarried woman was the rightful proprietor and guardian. Marriage could be contracted by paying some wealth to the woman's father or her kin. The Mahr was not paid to the wife for her protection, as had been provided in the Koran. An Arab desiring a noble offspring could lend his wife to a friend or a wealthy man. In other words, the wife was like a property of the husband and had the right to enjoy or dispose of in any way he liked. There was no regard for chastity. The rules relating to divorce were loose and were loaded in favour of men. It was not uncommon to observe the practice of female infanticide.

The Koranic Provisions

When the provisions made in the Koran are placed in this historical context, the religion of Islam meant significant improvements in the plight of women which was deplorable indeed.

- Polygamy was limited to four wives, preferably to one.
- The bride-price or Mahr was for the protection of the wife and was not to be paid to her father or her kin.
- She was to have definite claims to the inheritance left by her deceased husband and also her parents.
- She had a right to ask for divorce.
- She was not to be forced into a marriage and her consent was made an essential requirement.
- Marriage was made into a contract and she was not to be deprived of the Mahr in the event that the husband wanted to marry again.
- Widow remarriage was explicitly permitted.
- Infanticide of females was forbidden (Hadith, Vol. 3, No.591)
- Motherhood was glorified ("Paradise lies at the feet of those who respect their mother").

All these effected significant improvements in the status of women when compared with the Pre-Islamic Arab world.

An Alternative View

A different view of the status of women in Islam has been presented by many scholars in recent years. It is acknowledged that with the founding of Islam, the position of women improved but it is unreasonable to claim that Islam and the Islamic Law (*Shariat*) place woman on the same footing as man. It is contended that the treatment of women in Islam reflects the culture of a patriarchal and male-dominated society. In their view Islam needs not a revival but a reformation as most other religions of the world have gone through at one time or another in the process of their evolution and development.

A few instances are quoted below. For a more detailed discussion, see Anwar Hekmat, *Women and the Koran,* 1997 ; Fatima Mernissi, *Beyond the Veil,* 1987 ; G.R. Driver and J.C. Miles, *The Assyrian Laws,* 1935 (quoted in Hekmat) ; Wiebke Walter, *Women in Islam,* 1993 ; Irshad Manji, *The Trouble With Islam,* Random House, 2003.

- Created Unequal

  Many scholars quote the Koran to point out the inequality between men and women as one of the cardinal principles of the Koran. " Men are the protectors and maintainers of women, because Allah has made one of them to excel the other. ...Therefore, the righteous women are devoutly obedient (to Allah and to their husbands)..."Koran (4 : 34).

- Polygamy

  Some scholars have also been critical of Islam from the point of view of inequity to women due to polygamy permitted to men but polyandry denied to women. (Fatima Mernissi, *Beyond the Veil,* 1987)

- Religion

  A man and a woman are treated in a discriminatory manner when it comes to a Muslim marrying a non-Muslim. As one writer says,
  " Although a man is allowed to marry a non-Muslim woman, the woman is totally prohibited from marrying any non-Muslim man."
  " The divine law is made in the man's favor ; the woman is disadvantaged." Two surahs from the Koran are quoted to support this, Koran 2: 221 and Koran 5:5.

• Bride Price

Some commentators point out that the Mahr essentially
constitutes a purchase price for a woman and " Islam
considers the woman as a commodity, and her price is
determined by her position." (Anwar Hekmat, *Women and the
Koran* , p117). Some scholars trace the Islamic custom of
bride price to the ancient Assyrian word *mahiru*, meaning
price. The same source traces the Mahr to the ancient Code
of Hammurabi, prevalent in the ancient Arab world. For
details, see G.R. Driver and J.C. Miles, *The Assyrian Laws*,
1935 quoted in Hekmat, ibid. p.119). Hekmat concludes that
Mahr was a continuation of the ancient system in which an
unmarried girl was the property of her father and "marriage
in Islam is merely a sales transaction".

• Inheritance
Although a woman is recognized as one having a right to
inheritance to her deceased husband's and her parents'
properties, her shares are smaller than that of a male heir.
"….the male will have twice the share of the female." (Koran
6 : 5: 176).

• Crime and Punishment
Many researchers also point out that women are much more
vulnerable under the Islamic law than men. For the same
kinds of misconduct, women are handed more severe
punishments than men. For details, see Wiebke Walter,
Women in Islam, 1993.

• Value of Female Witness
Some feminist scholars also find it unacceptable and
discriminatory that the evidential value of a female witness is
considered to be less than that of a man. Two female
witnesses are to be counted as the equivalent of one male
witness (Koran 2:282).

Chapter 6

Sikh Marriage

6.1 Background and Founding of the Sikh Religion

- The founder of the Sikh religion was Nanak (1469-1539), the first of ten Sikh gurus, or prophets. After his enlightenment he came to be known as Guru Nanak. Nanak was born in a Hindu family in a village in India , near the city of Lahore, now in Pakistan. Some time in his late 20s or early 30s Nanak experienced a religious calling, while wandering about in search of enlightenment. Sikh in Punjabi language means a disciple ('shishya'). One who became a disciple of Guru Nanak, the founder of the Sikh faith, came to be called a Sikh.

- Nanak's teachings are collected in the Sikh scriptures, known as *Guru Granth Sahib*, a large collection of hymns---prayers, praises for God, admonitions, and benedictions.

Instead of footnotes, some details are placed at the end of the book under the title " Miscellaneous Notes" (MN---numbered).

6.2 The Essence of the Sikh Religion

- In Nanak's time, Hinduism had become highly ritualistic and rigid and the caste system was becoming a divisive force. Islam was becoming intolerant and forcible conversion was becoming common. Nanak, like another liberal saint, Kabir (1440-1518) endeavoured to synthesize the elements of Islam and Hinduism.

- Nanak rejected the caste system and ritualistic elements of Hinduism. He took the Hindu principle of 'karma' and reincarnation. From Islam, he took the teaching that there is but one God. Thus the Sikh religion can be aptly described as a synthesis of Hinduism and Islam.

Later Developments

- Nanak made pacifism and compassion the cornerstone of the Sikh religion. In contrast to the original teachings of Nanak, Sikhs in their later history, became known as the most militant of warriors. The fifth Guru, Arjan Dev (1581-1606) introduced the militant aspect in self defence against the atrocities of the Mughal rulers.
- The last of the Sikh gurus, Gobind Singh (1675-1708) organized the militant force known as *Singhs* (lions).
- They were to be identifiable and distinguishable from their dress (five K's) : They were to wear 'Kes' (long hair), 'Kanga' (comb), 'Kachk' (short trouser), 'Kara' (steel bracelet), and 'Kirpan' (steel dagger).
- The last Guru also established the tradition that there was to be no Sikh Guru in human form---the Granth was to be regarded as the final Sikh Guru.
- For the reason mentioned in the last bullet, wedding vows are taken in front of the Guru Granth Sahib, and not in front of any image or idol.

The Sikhs number about 20 million worldwide. Sikhs are concentrated in the Punjab region of India. Sikh communities are also found in large numbers in England, Southeast Asia and North America.

Under the Sikh faith, the marriage ceremony (called *anand karaj*) is also relatively simple like a Muslim marriage and emphasizes spirituality. It is not a contract. It is a formal announcement of the spiritual bond between a man and a woman. In the native Punjabi language, *anand karaj* literally means "Ceremony of Bliss".

6.3 Sikh Marriage Customs

Engagement

The customs that the Sikhs follow are similar to a Punjabi wedding in varying degrees (see Punjabi Wedding) except the religious ceremony (described below).

Traditionally, among the Sikhs as in other religious followers in India, a marriage is arranged by the parents of the two sides. Generally a formal engagement takes place, though not mandatory.

An engagement ceremony is a simple one. In the presence of the Guru Granth Sahib, the bride's messenger and the bridegroom's family exchange gifts for the bride and bridegroom at the bride's home. Prayers are sung from the Granth sahib and the congregation invokes blessings of God for the betrothed couple. After this, *karah parshad*, sacred food is distributed among members of the gathering. A formal betrothal ceremony is not mandatory, however. A Sikh wedding can be solemnenized without a previous betrothal. Also a Sikh wedding can take place on any day---unlike a Hindu marriage where an auspicious day is prescribed. However, a birthday of one the ten Gurus is preferred as the wedding day.

The marriage procession, as is customary in Punjab, arrives with the groom, his parents, other family members and friends . In olden days it was customary for the groom to come on a horse. In modern days quite often he comes in a beautifully decorated car. When they reach the bride's house, members of the groom's party participate in singing and dancing---the groom's parents are expected to take an active part in it to express their happiness on the occasion.

Milni

When the groom's party arrives, they are formally welcomed by the bride's family. This is called *Milni*, meaning the union. The two sides introduce themselves and exchange garlands. The gathering is treated with drinks, sweets and snacks.

In traditional families, some stanzas are sung at this time from the Holy Scripture (called *Shabad*). The following *Shabad* is quite popular which reads as follows :
"Friends have come to our house.
The True One
Has brought us together.
The union is pleasing to God.
In the union of hearts
Is the seed of happiness and peace.
The house is made beautiful ;
It rings with music,
And with soundless sound,
Friends have come to our house."

The groom is then taken inside the house and women welcome him with traditional folk songs.

6.4 Sikh Wedding Ceremony

For many years, Sikhs were considered by the Hindu community to be a sect of the Hindu faith. The ceremony was solemnised by the Hindu Brahmins and the traditional Vedic rites were performed. Islam originated as a reaction to paganism in the Middle East. Various forms of idolatry came to be associated with paganism and the religious practices became highly ritualistic to the point of losing the inner meaning.
The Sikh religion in India also developed as a reaction against the rigidity of the caste system and rituals becoming more important than the real spirit of religion.

Anand Karaj

The Vedic rites were replaced by the Sikh wedding ceremony, *Anand Karaj*. Anand Karaj as the wedding ceremony was introduced by Guru Amar Das (1552) although the four Lavans (see below) were composed by his successor Guru Ram Das Ji (fourth Guru of the ten Gurus of the Sikh faith).

Under social pressure from the Sikh community, legislation for recognition of Anand Karaj as the official religious ceremony under the Sikh faith was passed only recently in 1909.

The following provides a description of the Sikh wedding ceremony which normally takes place in a Sikh temple (*Gurdwara*) . It could also take place in the bride's house but it must be in the presence of the holy scripture.

- A copy of the Guru Granth Sahib is the centre of the ceremony. The priest asks the couple to take seats in front of the Holy Scripture with the bride sitting on the left hand side of the bridegroom. As a mark of respect to the Holy Scripture, the bride and the bridegroom as well as all attending the ceremony are required to cover their heads with a piece of cloth.

- The priest explains to the couple the Sikh concept of marriage---marriage means forging a spiritual bond between them with Guru as the witness.

The following are some selected stanzas that the priest recites and the *ragis* (professional singer devotees) sing :

"The bride should think of
No other man
Except her husband ;
So the Guru ordains.

She alone is of good family,
She shines with light,
Who is adorned
With the love of her husband.

They who sit together
Are not husband and wife,

But they whose spirits
Have fused into a single flame.

A loaf of dry bread,
Bare earth for bed
With the beloved
Is full of happiness."

"Other person's property,
Another man's wife,
Evil-speaking of another
Poison life.
Thought of another man's wife
Is like the touch
Of a poisonous snake."

- The priest asks the couple to affirm that they understand this and that both of them understand and accept the duties of married life. Each is required to signify that they agree to these conditions by nodding the head.
- Prayer.

The wedding ceremony begins with prayers (*ardas*) from the Holy scripture. These are sung by the *ragis*.

- Ceremonial Shawl *(Paala)*.

Paala is the shawl folded lengthwise which links the couple throughout the marriage ceremony. The devotional singers (*ragis*) sing some select verses from the Holy scripture as the shawl is being placed over the shoulder of the groom. The right end is placed in his hands and the left end is given to the bride to hold, by her father or the one acting in that capacity.

This is a variation of what is commonly known in Christian , Hindu and other marriage ceremonies as Tying the Knot.

Four Rounds (*Laavan*)

There are four Laavans or stanzas from the Holy scripture which are recited by the priest and are also sung by the singers. These are parts of the Guru Granth Sahib.

These Lavaans were composed by Sri Guru Ram Das Ji (the fourth Guru of the ten Gurus of Sikh faith), as mentioned earlier. It is believed that he composed these nuptial rounds for his son's wedding in 1610 and these have become almost mandatory since then.

The Lavaans (Hymns of Marriage)

Lavaan One :
The priest reads or sings the First Round and the couple rises and slowly and meditatively walks clockwise around the Guru Granth Sahib. The round must be taken clockwise to signify moving with time and not against it. A common practice is for close family members such as brothers and sisters and cousins to stand behind and hold the couple's hands and help them take rounds. After each round, the bride and the bridegroom bow before the Holy scripture.

Each Laavan starts with the invocation, " God, I am obliged to You for your grace". The original texts of these are reproduced in Miscellaneous Notes [MN-22].

The first Lavaan thanks God for providing the devotee guidance of the Guru who engaged him to love the Lord. This is the beginning of the marriage of the soul with God and declares the path of duty. God ordains the performance of duty and declares *the path of duty.*

Lavaan Two :
The teacher speaks of the omnipresence of God
And reveals to the disciple
The knowledge of the divine.
The fear of the fearless enters the mind
And the *dirt of egotism vanishes.*

The Lord Himself pervades everything,
Within and without is one God.
In the second round
The song of the soul is heard.

Lavaan Three :
In the third round
Mind is freed from material attachment.
In the company of saints
God himself is found---
The pure and omnipresent God.
In the heart the sound of the divine name echoes.
In the third round,
The disciple of Nanak says,
The mind awakens with detachment.

Lavaan Four :
In the fourth round,
Mind becomes peaceful ;
The self is realized.
The Lord is united with His bride ;
The bride is full of bliss,
With her heart filled with His name,
The disciple of Nanak says,
In the fourth round is found
The omnipresent and immortal God.

With the fourth round, the union with the divine spirit is
complete and this union becomes the source of eternal bliss for
the couple. According to the Sikh Codes of Conduct the couple
has been officially married by the Guru at this point.

- Blessing (*Shagan*) with Flower Petals
  To bless and congratulate the newly wed couple, the
  congregation (*sadh sangat*) showers flower petals on the
  couple. It is recommended by the traditionalists that flower
  petals be not showered in the presence of the Guru Granth

Sahib but at a separate place lest it should mean disrespect to the Guru. It has also become customary for the guests to give money to the bride and bridegroom which is donated to charity.

- *Lungar*

At the conclusion of the wedding ceremony, guests are served food (*lungar*). A Sikh marriage ceremony is open to all and one need not have a formal invitation to attend it. It is desirable that the food that is served at the conclusion of the ceremony be simple and not an ostentatious display of one's wealth. A more formal reception may be held later at a different place.

Emphasis on simplicity is understandable in the light of the purpose of the Sikh religion---to eliminate distinction between castes and classes of any type.

Chapter 7

Buddhist Marriage

7.1 Background and Founding of Buddhism

- Buddhism was founded by Gautama Siddharta (563-483 B.C.) , a royal prince born in the 6th century B.C. in Nepal. He came to be known as Gautama Buddha (Enlightened One) after attaining enlightenment in India.
- The disciples of Buddha wrote the teachings of Buddha in texts known as *Tripitaka.*

Instead of footnotes, some details are placed at the end of the book under the title " Miscellaneous Notes" (MN---numbered).

7.2 The Essence of the Buddhist Philosophy

- Sorrows are caused by the endless cycle of birth and death. The cycle of birth and death is caused by "desire", "thirst", or "craving". The way to be free from this cycle (to attain Nirvana) is to conquer desire by following a moral code of conduct. The five basic rules of moral conduct are : abstain from killing, stealing, telling lies, improper sexual conduct, and intoxicants.
- A major distinction between Hinduism and Buddhism is that Buddha rejected the hierarchical caste system of the Vedic scriptures.

Development of Buddhism

- The world population of the Buddhist faith is about 310 million. For several centuries under the patronage of several Indian kings Buddhism flourished in India. The royal

patronage reached its zenith with King Asoka (3rd century
B.C.) of the Mauryan empire).

After witnessing the massacre in the Kalinga War in which he
came out victorious, King Asoka relinquished violence and
warfare. He sent Buddhist missionaries to spread the teachings of
Buddha to many countries of South Asia and Southeast Asia.
Buddhism became the major religion in Sri Lanka, Thailand,
Burma, Indonesian islands of Sumatra, Java, Bali, Japan, China,
Korea, and Tibet. But strangely enough, in India, the birthplace
of Buddhism, there was no growth in the number of followers.
The main reason was that Hinduism absorbed Buddhism within
its fold by saying that Buddha was in fact an incarnation of the
Hindu god Vishnu. In many ways the Buddhist faith became
indistinguishable from the Hindu faith and in the same way,
when Buddhist missionaries entered a new country they did not
ask the natives to give up their old gods. This has, however, acted
as a catalyst for a revival of Buddhism in the West in recent
decades.

- In the twentieth century Buddhism has begun to revive and
  grow again especially in the Western world---largely because
  of its universal appeal of peace and nonviolence. In the age of
  meaningless devastation and misery wrought by nuclear
  power, and disenchantment with excessive material progress
  resulting in a threat to environment, the American Buddhism
  has assumed a new identity and importance.
- There are two major sects of Buddhism, Hinayana and
  Mahayana [MN-14]. Hinayana ("the small vehicle") is the
  more orthodox sect of Buddhism of which Theravada is the
  major school. Mahayana ("the large vehicle") is the larger
  and more liberal segment. It allows for absorption of new
  ideas and interpretations of the original teachings of Buddha.
  Buddha himself opened a door to this development by
  modestly suggesting that he had found only a handful of
  truths and there might be many others.

7.3 Wedding Customs and Ceremony

- Buddha did not prescribe any custom or ritual to be followed for marriage. He taught the virtues that man and woman should have mutual respect for one another. The partners should have pure and selfless love for one another and help one another in the attainment of the ultimate goal of human life, attainment of 'Nirvana', which is freedom from the bondage of cycle of birth and death.

Indian Buddhist Wedding Ceremony

- In India, the Buddhist wedding ceremony is very simple. The following aspects of the ceremony are commonly observed and variations are small, if any :
- Since Buddhism did not accept the authority of the Vedas, there are no Vedic rites as are followed in all Hindu marriages. The Vedic verses are, therefore, not recited. There is no encircling of the fire or 'Sapta-padi' (seven steps / vows).
- Even though Buddhism recognized several Hindu deities, Hindu gods and goddesses are not invoked. Instead, prayers are offered to Lord Buddha for the happiness of the union of man and woman.
- Lotus as the symbol of purity, incense as the material to ward off evil spirits, and decorative lamps as symbol of wisdom--- all figure prominently in the Indian Buddhist wedding ceremonies.
- Wedding normally takes place in a Buddhist temple. A monk may solemnize a Buddhist wedding but an officiating monk is not necessary. This is because according to the Buddhist philosophy, marriage is a social institution and not a religious sacrament as in other religions. Any respectable person well-versed in Buddhist scriptures is acceptable as the one solemnizing the marriage. The monk puts a fresh leaf into an urn containing water with the chanting of the *Heart of Wisdom*

Sutra. The water is thus believed to become holy. Three drops of water are put on the foreheads of the bride and groom. The monk then cleanses the water off their foreheads with a wooden spoon to symbolize the cleansing of the mind.

• The bride and the groom sit side by side in front of the officiating monk. The bride and groom are asked to exchange lotus and incense. The exchange symbolizes that they give a solemn promise to one another to be considerate, loving, respectful, and faithful to one another.

Sometime the monk may read out and recite some verses from the Buddhist sacred books which explain the basic Buddhist philosophy and counsel that they should strive together to fulfill the goal of life, attainment of *Nirvana*, through Right Thoughts and Right Actions (Eightfold Path prescribed by Buddha). A common benediction piece called *Pansil* (Five Rules of Morality) is used to seek refuge in Lord Buddha and to take five vows. Other popular pieces that are used for the wedding ceremony are discourses on the reciprocal duties of the husband and wife as explained by Buddha in the *Sigala Sutta* and could include the Buddhist story of Nakulapita (the husband) and Nakulamata (the wife) who symbolized pure love between a husband and wife. This completes the wedding.

• After this the two offer lotus and incense to the image of the Buddha and seek blessings from the monks present at the ceremony. Several selected guests are designated to come near the seat of the bride and groom and light a lamp to pray to Lord Buddha to give them wisdom so that their conjugal life becomes happy and blissful.

• A Buddhist scholar notes that when a Buddhist offers flowers or lights a lamp, it does not represent idol worship. These are not rites or rituals. The "flowers that soon fade, and the flames that die down speak to him of the impermanency of all conditioned things. The image serves him as an object for concentration…endeavours to emulate the qualities of the Master." For a short but authentic description of the Buddhist wedding ceremony in India and Sri Lanka, see

Piyadassi Thero, *The Spectrum of Buddhism*, Publisher Jivinda De Silva, New York, 1991.

- The ceremony is followed by a feast at the bride's home or at a suitable rented place. Feeding the monks and giving them gift of robes and other necessities of life to extend support to the Sangha (Buddhist monastry) is also a part of the event.

7.4 Buddhist Weddings Outside India

The Buddhist wedding ceremony is quite different in other countries where Buddhism flourished, namely, Sri Lanka, Thailand, Japan, Korea, and China. The wedding ceremonies in those countries have incorporated many aspects of the native culture and tradition. For specific details, see Robert C. Lester, *Buddhism : The Path to Nirvana*, Harper and Row, 1987.

Thai Wedding

- In Thailand, for instance, in the traditional Buddhist families especially in the rural society, marriage by service is quite common. The groom lives in bride's house and has to provide service to the future father-in-law to win the bride's hands in marriage.
- A traditional Buddhist wedding ceremony in Thailand starts with a ceremony called "sukhwan" (calling the vital forces). A conical structure with rice and flowers is built on a large tray with a candle at the head of the cone. This ceremonial cone is the house of vital forces which are invoked to pave the transition of the bride and the groom from a single status to the married status with its privileges and responsibilities.

Japanese Wedding

As is well known, the people of Japan are fond of respecting and observing   their old customs and traditions. Yet in contemporary marriage customs and wedding ceremonies, they have imbibed the religious and cultural traditions of other countries because of its colorful history.

Japanese wedding ceremonies are a combination of Shinto religion, Buddhist tradition, and modern Western culture. Spring and Fall are very popular as wedding seasons in Japan. On lucky days in those seasons, many shrines, churches, ceremony halls and hotels are full of guests who are invited to weddings.

Traditional pre-wedding events, which are called "Yui-no", are still important for many Japanese people, especially for people those who live in the rural areas of Japan. "Yui-no" in essence means celebrating the union of two families by dining together before the wedding takes place. A few months before the wedding ceremony, the two families of future bridegroom and bride meet at a dinner and exchange gifts that include some items of happiness and fortune. Traditionally, the bride's family hosts this dinner and the future bride is expected to cook and give a show of her culinary skills. Several types of dried fish and fruits are exchanged which are considered as symbols of happiness since they were valuable foods in the old days. An essential item consists of folding paper fan signifying happiness that will spread out in the future. Some traditional families include cherry blossoms as essential for wishing beautiful children being born as a result of the union. Another important item consists of Kimono, the traditional Japanese wedding outfit for the bride. Some couples add engagement rings to these items.

- Shinto (which literally means 'the way of gods') is the indigenous faith of the Japanese people and it is as old as Japan itself. Shinto is a loosely organized native religion and consists of a large variety of beliefs and practices. Shinto gods are called *kami*. They are sacred spirits which take the form of things and concepts important to life, such as wind, rain, mountains, trees, rivers and fertility. Humans become kami after they die and are revered by their families as ancestral kami. The kami of extraordinary people are even enshrined at some shrines.

- From the fourth century and onwards, Japan came under the influence of Buddhism from China and Korea. Shinto religious beliefs and practices became interwoven with Buddhism.

- With the passage of time, the boundaries between the two religions became less and less distinct. Thus for historical reasons, the wedding ceremonies in Japan reflect the Shinto tradition as well as the Buddhist religious practices. Shinto venerates kami, the spirits that inhabit the entire earth. Every crop and every village has its own kami, and every ancestor is a kami. So the soul of the Shinto wedding ceremony is honoring these spirits and asking for their blessing for a happy and harmonious married life for the new couple.

- But with greater contacts with the West, marriage customs and wedding ceremonies show some Western influences, although culturally the Japanese people are greatly attached to their tradition. The old customs of arranged marriage are gradually giving place to courtship. Yet parental approval plays an important role in marriage negotiations. A matchmaker or go-between ('Nakodo') who could be a family priest or friend is often used for marriage negotiations. Bridal dowry, an old custom in marriages, is becoming less common. The role of women in social and economic life is becoming more diversified. Exchanging rings, cutting a cake at the wedding ceremony and the custom of going on a honeymoon are becoming common.

The wedding ceremony consists of rituals ---purification, prayer, invocation, and offering mixed with the ring exchange, recitation of wedding vows, and the sharing of 'saki' cups.

The following are the major steps in a Japanese wedding ceremony :

- The bride and groom are seated facing the Shinto sanctuary.

- The celebrant priest begins with a prayer. He then presents an offering of food and drink to the kami.
- The priest performs a ritual purification of all those present by waving a branch called the 'harai-gushi'. Chanting to the gods, he asks them to bless the bride and groom.
- Sharing of 'Saki' cups by the newly married couple is the most important part of the Japanese wedding ceremony. Accompanied by loud flute music, three maiden girls bring three cups of Saki. The Saki is offered first to the groom sitting in one table with his friends and relatives. He sips it three times and then it is taken to the bride's table who sips from the same cup three times. This is done separately with three cups. This is known as "three, three, nine times" ('San-san-ku-do') . Nine is believed to be a lucky number according to Japanese mythology. The maiden girls then serve Saki to all others seated in other tables. The priest instructs the assembly to pick up their glasses and utter words of congratulations ('Omedeto Gozaimasu') to the new couple.
- In the American Buddhist community, the Western and Christian traditions are followed including exchange of rings and cutting of the wedding cake.

7.5 Women In Buddhism

Did women enjoy a more respectable position in the family and social life under Buddhism than under Hinduism or Islam ? This is a complex question and there are no easy answers. Discussion of these in the present context is limited to certain observations. This section on women in Buddhism has drawn heavily from Swarna de Silva, *The Place of Women in Buddhism*, Midlands Buddhist Society, UK, 1988.

Buddhism does not take institutions such as marriage where the position of women is important as a religious "sacrament" (as Hinduism, Christianity, or Islam does). The Buddhist position was that these matters were to be regulated by society through some kind of social, political, or legal process. The only requirement was that such arrangements were not be in fundamental conflict with the

'Dhamma'. Buddha's teaching was primarily concerned with individual spiritual emancipation and gender was not of much importance. However, the position of women under Buddhism was at best ambiguous and ambivalent. Sometimes the Buddha's views happened to coincide with commonly accepted contemporary social principles, sometimes they were contrary to these views.

- In the *Sigalovada Sutta,* the Buddha emphasizes the principle of reciprocity---with regard to the duties of wife to husband and vice versa. The equal burden of responsibility and duty laid on both husband and wife is the hall-mark of the Buddha's attitude to the role of women in family life. In this Sutta, the Buddha identifies qualities of women (beauty, sons, fidelity, virtue) which would make them the superior partner in a marriage, but these qualities are those that were generally accepted in the Buddha's time.

Every religion has jealously guarded entry into its innermost sanctum. In many religions the doors of this sanctum are barred to women, even to this day. The Buddha established the Bhikkhuni Order (monastry for women). According to some scholars establishment of an Order for women was a landmark in Buddhist and Indian history. That there was no discrimination based on sexes is evidenced by the Buddha's utterance in one of the verses:

" This is the vehicle
Be it a woman or be it a man
The one who takes this vehicle
Can attain the peace of Nibbana".

- At other places in the Buddhist canonical literature there are references to the position of females that the modern exponents of women liberation would find offensive. The *Dhaniya Sutta* extols obedience in wives reminding us of the Christian marriage imposed on wives to "obey" their husbands. Also, there are lists of kinds of wives that appear in the *Vinaya* and *Sutta Pitaka* with occasional hints that the more docile the kind of wife the better.

- Some Buddhist scholars have assessed the position of women in Buddhism by comparing their place in Buddhism with that in other religions. It is pointed out, for instance, that women cannot still officiate as priests under Hinduism. Similarly, Christianity has traditionally been a male-dominated religion without any clear position on the ordination of women as priests even today. In Islam too, women are denied full access to religious functions, and in some countries even access to the mosque.

Chapter 8

Jain Marriage

8.1 Background and Founding of Jainism

Mahavira is traditionally identified as the founder of Jainism. He was
a contemporary of the Buddha, Lao-tzu, and the Hebrew prophets of
the 6th century B.C.(Jeremiah and Ezekiel). Mahavir was, like
Guatama Buddha son of a royal household and lived a life of luxury.
Having become disenchanted with this kind of life, he renounced the
life of luxury and embraced asceticism. After twelve years of harsh
asceticism and meditation, he attained liberation ('moksha'). He
came to be known to his followers as *jina*, conqueror of the endless
cycle of birth and death, and hence the name of the religion "Jain".

Instead of footnotes, some details are placed at the end of the
book under the title " Miscellaneous Notes" (MN---numbered).

8.2 Jain Wedding Ceremony

Colour, folklore and songs dominate the celebrations of a typical
Rajasthani Jain wedding. In earlier times the festivities carried on for
weeks but today, they last for a period of 5 to 7 days.
Khol Bharna :
   This is the engagement ceremony in Rajasthani Jain wedding. The
   wedding rituals begin with Modi tying, marked by the tying of a
   religious thread around the wrists of the family members. Then
   the groom's sister performs a prayer. Pethi and mehndi are
   applied on the groom's hands for five days.
Ganesh Puja :
   Performed to ensure the wedding takes place without a mishap.
Kakandora

Then in a ritual called *Kakandora*, the groom's procession goes to the bride's house. The arrival of *Barat* at the marriage hall is known as *Pokhna*.

Maaya Bithana

The actual wedding rituals begin with *Maaya Bithana*. Mehndi is applied to the palms of the bride and groom and their hands are joined in 'hast-milap'.

No Fire Ritual

The followers of Jainism whose wedding ceremony is very similar in almost all respects to the Hindu ceremony do not lit fire. They believe in non-violence and are expected not to kill any living being. Lighting fire for the ceremony could attract insects that could get killed and hence they omit this part of the Hindu wedding ceremony.

Chapter 9

Zoroastrian (Parsi) Marriage

9.1 Background and Founding of Zoroastrianism

- The Parsis are followers of Zoroastrianism that originated in Persia
  (now Iran). They fled Persia in the 9th century and migrated to India due to the persecution of those that did not convert to Islam. They settled in India and were called by the local inhabitants , Parsis, the people from Persia. A large majority of them belonged to the business class and settled down in Bombay and Calcutta, two important centres of commerce.
- Though strictly speaking, they are not Hindus, they share a long cultural tradition with the Hindu population. The total world population of the Parsis is estimated to be between 150,000 to 200,000(100,000 in India). Although their numbers are not very large they have maintained their distinctive religious identity. They have contributed enormously to Indian industry and entrepreneurship. The names of the author and economist Dadabhai Naoroji, and of industrialists Jamshedji Tata, and JRD Tata stand out prominently.

Instead of footnotes, some details are placed at the end of the book under the title " Miscellaneous Notes" (MN---numbered).

9.2 The Essence of Zoroastrianism

- About 3,000 years ago, Zarathustra, founder of this monotheistic faith preached that there is only one God whom he called Ahura Mazda, Lord of Wisdom. The Zoroastrians consider fire to be sacred as other elements of Nature.

- The holy text of the Zoroastrians is the *Avesta*, composed in a language belonging to the early Iranian group of languages and resembling the language of the Vedas. The daily prayer-book the Parsis use everyday is *Khordeh Avesta* (the smaller Avesta). The *Videvat* are religious law books laying down codes of conduct and procedures for penance. The *Yasna* is the handbook of ceremonies and rituals etc, including the *Gathas* .
Some salient features of the Zoroastrian faith are :
- worship in fire temples (which contain nothing remarkable except a vase of sandalwood kept perpetually alight);
- praying on the sea shore to the rising and setting sun; celebration of marriages in public assembly;
- exposure of their dead to birds of prey for food , in what are called "towers of silence" (suggesting that even the mortal body should be used for the benefit of others) ;
- exclusiveness as regards marriage (no intermarriage); and
- the rule of covering the head in worship.
- The principal and cardinal virtue for the followers of Zarathustra is to adhere to the Zoroastrian creed of *Humata, Hukta, and Havarashtra*---good thoughts, good words, and good deeds.
- The followers of Zaratrhustra (known as Zarathrusti's) do not advocate conversion. They believe in increasing their numbers through more children and discourage inter-marriage (like the Jews, Catholics, and Muslims).
- All followers of Zoroastrianism have to wear the *Sadra* and *Kusti*, a narrow band round the waist, similar to the sacred thread of the Hindu Brahmins. *Aiwayaonhana* (which also means stormy sky) is the term used to refer to it in the Avesta. The band is woven out of 72 strands of sheep wool (symbolic of the 72 chapters of the Yasna) and is wound thrice round the waist symbolising the three cardinal tenets of the faith: good thoughts, good deeds and good words.

9.3   Parsi Wedding Ceremony

It is difficult to determine how many, and which, of their marriage customs are originally Zoroastrian or Persian, and how many, and which, are taken from their sister communities of India.

The Parsi wedding ceremony begins with the engagement, where the rings are exchanged and gifts are given. Then a ritual called *Mandav Saro* follows, a ceremony that begins four days before the wedding, to pray that the wedding proceeds without any obstacle.

Then in a ritual called *Divo Adarni*, the groom visits the bride's place with gifts and the actual wedding rituals commence with a ceremony called *Lagan*, which is an elaborate affair that concludes with the bride and groom accepting each other.

The bride and the bridegroom are at first made to sit opposite each other, separated by a piece of cloth held between them by two persons as a curtain, so that they may not see each other. Their hands are joined and the curtain is held over the hands. It is dropped after the hand-fastening ceremony. This part of the ritual signifies that the separation which hitherto existed between them, no longer exists now, and that they are now united in the bond of matrimony. As long as the curtain is held between them, they sit opposite each other, but on its removal, they are made to sit side by side. This also signifies that they, who were separate upto then, are now united together.

The wedding is soleminzed by two priests who stand before the couple and recite benedictions. The priests ask the couple, not once but three times, if they are entering into matrimony out of their own free will. A ceremonial fire is lit as witness to this ceremony. Note that Zoroastrians were and still are fire worshippers.

Ahunar and other Prayers

- The priests recite "Ahunar", considered to be the most holy prayer in the Zoroastrian religion. This prayer reads as follows :

"The will of the Lord is the law of righteousness.

The gifts of Vohu-mano to the deeds done in this world for Mazda.
He who relieves the poor makes Ahura king."
"May the year be auspicious, the day fortunate, the month
propitious in all these years and days and months!"

"For many years keep them worthy to perform worship
and utter prayers, to give charity and offerings, being just.
May they have health to fulfill all their duties! May they be liberal,
kind and good!
In the name of Ahura Mazda may both of you experience joy and
progress in life.". For the original texts, see [MN-28] and [MN-29].

"I say (these) words to you, marrying brides and bridegrooms!
Impress then upon your mind: May you two enjoy the life of good
mind by following the laws of religion. Let each one of you clothe the
other with righteousness. Then assuredly there will be a happy life for
you." - *Yasna* 53.5. (Quoted in Jivanji Jamshedji Modi, *Marriage
Customs Among the Parsis*).

- "Think of nothing but the truth, speak nothing but the truth,
  do nothing but what is proper—Shun all bad thoughts, shun
  all bad words, shun all bad deeds"
- "Recognize Ahura Mazda , the omniscient Lord and
  Zarathustra as your spiritual leader"

Throughout the invocation, prayer, and benedictions, the couple is
showered with rice and flower petals. Evidently, rice signifies
prosperity as practised in many other religious ceremonies common
to an agrarian society. Flower petals represent the beauty of Nature.
As a Zoroastrian priest put it, it is a prayer to the Almighty that, "may
the couple be endowed with wealth and beauty of married life."

- After the above admonitions, a few benedictions are followed
  in which priest invokes the forefathers and ask for their
  blessings for the couple.

- This is followed by a short benediction known as *Doa Tan Dorosti* in which priests ask for happiness, wealth, good health, and a long married life to be bestowed on the couple.
- Upon completion of the above, the man and woman are declared husband and wife, and they exchange rings.
- Then in a ceremony called *Varbedu*, the groom gifts a cash envelope to the bride's sister. Then *Pagh Dhovanu* follows where the sister-in-law touches the groom's feet with milk. A grand dinner is offered to celebrate the wedding.

The above description of the Parsi wedding ceremony has drawn heavily from Jivanji Jamshedji Modi, *Marriage Customs Among the Parsis*.

Chapter 10

Christian Marriage

10.1 The Christian Faith

The majority of the global population (about 33 % of the world population of 6 billion) are of the Christian faith and are concentrated largely in the USA, Canada, South America, Europe, and in some African countries.

- Born in Bethlehem, to Mary and Joseph (who was a carpenter), Jesus Christ, a Jew by birth, spread the message of universal message of love and mercy. In the environment of the Roman Empire, his message acquired a unique force of its own. But the non-believers had him crucified after he had been betrayed to them by one of his own disciples. But he is believed to have risen from his grave and this Resurrection gave new strength to his other followers, who went on spreading his message.

- The Christians believe in a Trinity of God the Father, God the Son, and God the Holy Ghost. Their Holy Scripture, the Bible, is a collection of 73 books, divided into two sections: the Old Testament which corresponds to the Bible of Judaism and the New Testament which is entirely based on Christ's messages and teachings.

Instead of footnotes, some details are placed at the end of the book under the title " Miscellaneous Notes" (MN---numbered).

Major Christian Sects

There is a wide variety of Christian sects, the two major
denominations being the Roman Catholic and Protestant. Within
these two major sects, there are many sub-divisions that differ in
some small details.
The Protestant Christian faith emerged with the Reformation in
England and Germany. An essential difference between the Roman
Catholic and the Protestant faith is that the Roman Catholics
consider Church and the Pope as the supreme authority on religious
matters. The Protestants, on the other hand, believe that the
Scripture is the final authority, and the authority of the Church is
secondary. Another difference is that the Catholics are slightly more
ritualistic that the Protestants. This is reflected in the more elaborate
wedding ceremonies of the Catholics.

10.2 Marriage Customs in Biblical Times

The Bible gives some interesting glimpses of marriage customs and
ceremonies that were prevalent during the Biblical times (e.g.,
marriages of Isaac and Rebecca, and Ruth and Boaz) .
The creation of Eve was the genesis of marriage and the union of
man and woman in human society.
The Bible says that after God created light and darkness, plants, trees,
and birds, streams and rivers,

> "…The Lord God formed man from the dust of the ground
> and breathed into his nostrils the breath of life, and man
> became a living being." (Genesis, 2, 7)
> The word 'man' seems to have been derived from the
> Hebrew word *adamah* meaning ground. Thus he came to be
> called Adam.
> "Then Lord God said , 'it is not good for the man to be
> alone. I will make a helper suitable for him" . (Genesis, 2, 18)
> "Then the Lord God made a woman from the rib he had
> taken out of the man."

"The man said, this is now bone of my bone, and flesh of my flesh, she shall be called 'woman' for she was taken out of man."

Lord God said, "For this reason shall a man leave his father and mother , and be united to his wife : and they twain shall be one flesh".

(Genesis 2, 22-24)

Marriage of Isaac and Rebecca

The Biblical story of Isaac and Rebecca resembles in essence a typical modern day Jewish marriage.

It was customary for the father to arrange the son's and daughter's marriage . When Abraham decided that his son, Isaac has attained marriageable age , he sent a trusted servant to the city of Nahor to find a wife for Isaac. Abraham did not want that his son should be married to a local Canaanite (a tribe different from his). It was the preferred custom to marry within the clan to perpetuate and strengthen one's own clan.

There he met Isaac's cousin, Rebecca, and her father, Bethuel, and her brother, Laban. Bethuel and Laban gave their consent to Rebecca's marriage to Isaac.

The family sends a messenger with gifts of gold and silver to the mother and brother of Rebecca. This is reminiscent of the bride-price.

" He put the ring on her nose, and the bracelets on her hands" and this was the sign that Isaac's courtship was accepted.

The meeting of the bride and the groom is described as under :

" Isaac took her into his mother's tent, and she became his wife, and he loved her" (Genesis, xxiv)

Marriage of Jacob and Rachel

The story of Jacob and Rachel illustrates several social customs. It was customary to marry the eldest daughter first. Secondly, polygamy was quite common. Thirdly, if the bridegroom did not have the means to pay the price of a bride, he could earn the bride by working for the bride's father.

For Jacob it was love at first sight for Rachel. But he did not have the means to pay the bride-price. Jacob worked for seven years for Laban on his farm in order to earn the hand of his daughter, Rachel. He was tricked by Laban into marrying her older sister, Leah. With Leah's collusion, at the time of wedding, Laban substituted Leah in the bridal veil in place of Rachel. Jacob was unable to see her because of the veil. It would be noted that wearing a veil was common among married women in the Biblical times at the time of wedding and even after the wedding .

To justify the deceit, Laban cited the custom that the elder daughter must be married first. Soon after, Jacob married Rachel as well, illustrating that polygamy was legal in ancient Israel, but only wealthy men could afford several wives. Solomon's son, Rehoboam had 18 wives and 60 concubines.

Marriage of Ruth and Boaz

The Book of Ruth provides a fascinating glimpse into an interesting marriage custom of the ancient Israel. It illustrates the custom that in the event a brother dies leaving a widow but without a son , it becomes the duty of brother, if any to take responsibility of the dead brother's widow. The brother is expected to marry the widowed sister-in-law to perpetuate the family. If there is no other brother, a close relative should marry the widow.

It tells the story of a Moabite woman who married a Hebrew. After her husband died, she chose to devote her life to look after her widowed mother-in-law, Naomi, rather than return to her family in Moab.

Ruth and Naomi moved to Bethlehem where Ruth met , Boaz, a wealthy farmer and a kinsman of her late husband. They got married. These came to be known as "levirate" marriages(from the Latin word meaning husband's brother). In these marriages, the firstborn son would inherit the first husband's property, an important consideration in a society that resisted the loss of property to anyone outside the clan. Boaz married the widow Ruth and became the "kinsman-redeemer".

Boaz also acquired the property of Naomi and Ruth . Boaz said to the witnesses, "I have acquired Ruth as my wife in order to maintain the name of the dead with his property, so that his name will not disappear from among his family or town records. Today you are witnesses." (Book of Ruth iv, 9)

In ancient times in Israel, for redemption and transfer of property, one party took off his sandal and gave it to the other, the buyer. The story of Ruth and Boaz also shows the custom of giving one's shoes to surrender the right to ownership. This custom of presenting shoes to the new bridegroom is still prevalent and practiced among the traditional Arabs. This signifies the father (or his representative) giving away the right to his daughter.

Ruth and Boaz became the parents of a son, Obed, who was the grandfather of David, the celebrated king of Israel. Many generations later, Jesus was born in the same line.

Betrothal and Marriage

In Biblical times, betrothal represented an agreement that had the same legal weight as wedding. It was the duty of fathers to arrange the best possible matches for their children.

Marriage was a covenant between families. Marriages were arranged at an early age ----at the age of puberty for girls, 12 to 14.

After a father had chosen a wife for his son, he negotiated the amount of *mohar*, or the bride-price, a sum to be paid to the bride's father. From the Biblical accounts 50 shekels of silver (1 shekel equals 11.5 grams in metric measure) was a common bride-price. The formal betrothal ceremony took place before the witnesses and the father and groom paid at least a part of the *mohar* at this time. The rest was to be paid on the wedding day. The wedding sometime took place after twelve months or less during which period the daughter continued to live in her father's household.

The betrothed couple was considered to be husband and wife and be faithful to one another. The betrothal could be broken only by a formal divorce. Mary and Joseph were betrothed at the time of Jesus' birth, and Matthew calls them husband and wife.

Israel's laws were harsh against anyone who raped a betrothed woman. It was considered as adultery for which the penalty was death.

Sarah and Surrogate Mother

Abraham and Sarah had been married for 10 years. Even after 10 years, Sarah did not conceive. Realizing that Abraham was worried that his lineage would disappear without a son, Sarah gave his husband her Egyptian slave, Hagar, as a surrogate mother. A son, Ishmael, was born to Hagar.

Four of Israel's 12 tribes are also believed to have descended from slave women given to Jacob by two of his wives, Rachel and Leah, who could not conceive.

Rights of Divorce

The Babylonian laws (called the Code of Hammurabi) allowed a husband to divorce his wife simply by telling her "Thou art not my wife" and this had legal force. A woman's adultery or childlessness was a sufficient ground for a divorce.

The Law of Moses, however, required Jewish husbands to draw up a "bill of divorce", a public document that allowed the wife to marry any other man.

Jewish women did not have any right to initiate a divorce---except to desert him.

Although the Old testament permitted divorce, God was seen as frowning upon divorce : "For I hate divorce, says the Lord.... So take heed to yourselves and do not be faithless."

Jesus accepted adultery as a ground for divorce, when some disciples asked him if it was lawful to divorce one's wife for any reason" (Matthews, 19).

Song of Solomon

In the Song of Solomon (Old Testament), a detailed description of the bridal party and festivities can be obtained (Song of Songs,viii.2). The drink of honey, spiced wine and juice of pomegranate taken by the bride and the bridegroom mentioned here can be traced forward to several centuries. Many scholars consider these as fertility potions. In the New Testament, a wedding ceremony of Cana in Galilee is described that bears a close resemblance to a modern-day wedding among the Christians, Jews, and also Moslems. The lifting of the veil of the bride , and seeing her for the first time and loudly crying out in joy at the beauty of the bride is still prevalent among the Arabs and Bedouins as a ceremony.

No other religious scripture provides such a detailed descriptive account of marriage customs as the Bible does.

10.3 Early and Medieval Church Wedding

In the early Christian period, betrothal preceded the actual wedding and consisted of a mutual contract or written agreement between the two families that the future marriage of the couple would be performed within a specified time . This contract was confirmed by certain gifts or donations by the bride's family and often included landed property (called *arrae et arrabones*) . In addition, the contract was confirmed by a ring, a kiss, a dowry in writing, with a couple of witnesses. Any break of the promise after this incurred the censure of the Church and sometimes the penalty of law.

Presenting a ring as part of the ceremony was customary among the ancient Romans and the Jews. This was gradually admitted into Christian marriages. Historians show that in the time of Pope Nicholas (860 A.D), ring was to be used at the time of betrothal only but not at the actual wedding ceremony. But in the later period ring was used on both occasions.

The following rites were observed in a wedding ceremony in the Early and Medieval Church :

- The joining of the right hands of the couple
- The bridal veil was essential in bride's dress
- The woman was given away by her father or a relative
- The coronation of the couple with crowns of garlands to celebrate the union and symbolise victory
- The priest blessed the ring and gold coins placed on a shield with holy water. These were then presented by the groom to the bride saying : "With this ring I wed thee, with this gold I honour thee, with this gift I dowe thee"
- The bride then prostrated at the feet of the bridegroom and kissed the right foot of her spouse
- The priest would say the following prayer :
  " Let the yoke of love and of peace be upon her. Let her be lovely in the eyes of her husband as was Rachel, let her be wise as was Rebekah, let her live long and be faithful as was Sarah. let the author of mischief have no part in any of her doings".

It is noted that bride was still considered the property of the father and she was being transferred to the groom. Also, the bride was charged with all the responsibilities and duties for a happy married life.

10.4 The Rise of Civil Marriage

In the seventeenth century the wave of Reformation in Germany initiated and spearheaded by Martin Luther spread to England. It meant challenging the Papal authority of Rome. This resulted in the Civil Marriage Act of 1653. It prescribed a obligatory civil ceremony before a Justice of Peace consisting merely in the expression of mutual consent and the interlocking of hands (the old hand-fastening) but without the use of a ring. The marriage ceremony was thus taken out of the hands of the clergy and was recognised as a civil matter.

The other notable development was in 1836. A new Civil Marriage Act was passed which is still in force in England. This was followed as a model in most of Europe and later in North America. The religious rite was made optional and could be performed anywhere by a minister of any Christian sect . The only essential requirement was a simple civil contract in the presence of at least two witnesses. This forms the source of most Christian wedding ceremonies in the world today.

10.5 Protestant Wedding Ceremony

The bride is accompanied by her father or the guardian with flowergirls. The groom is accompanied by the bestman.
The following is a short description of steps in a Protestant wedding ceremony. The ceremony, prayers, and marriage vows are based on *The Book of Common Prayers* of the Church of England.

- Addressing the congregation
- Invocation
- Consent
- Invitation to block the marriage
- Wedding Vows
- Blessing and exchanging the rings
- Pronouncement of the husband and wife

A traditional Protestant wedding ceremony starts with the following opening words by the officiating minister :

" We have come together in the presence of God to witness and bless the joining together of...... and ....in Holy Matrimony. The bond and covenant of marriage was established by God in creation, and our Lord Jesus Christ adorned this manner of life by His presence and first miracle at a wedding in Cana of Galilee. It signifies to us the mystery of the union between Christ and His church, and the Holy Scripture commends it to be honoured among all people."

The invocation includes readings from the Bible and a sermon explaining the significance of marriage and its responsibilities.

Normally, consent of the father or guardian is an important aspect of the ceremony. The officiating minister asks the gathering " Who gives this woman to be married to this man ?" The father or someone representing him comes forward to say " I do". Many modern feminists object to this part of the ceremony as this treats the unmarried girl to be a property.

Sometimes the minister may ask : "if there is any just reason why the couple may not be married, speak now, or else forever hold your peace."

As in all wedding ceremonies, wedding vows are an important part and here wide variations are observed. In a traditional type of wedding vows, the bride and then the groom repeat separately after the minister :

> " In the name of God, I (name).....take you (name)...., to be (wife/husband) to have and to hold from this day forward, for better for worse, for richer for poorer, in sickness and in health, to love and to cherish, until we are parted by death."

Traditional wedding vows also contained the words for the bride " to obey". But in modern times, this is omitted.

Composing Wedding Vows

In modern times, many brides and grooms are beginning to compose their own wedding vows to reflect their personal emotions and thoughts. The practice has become particularly popular among those who are united through mixed and non-denominational marriages, and they desire changes in the traditional vows. Also, with the rising feminist trends, new brides wish to emphasize in their wedding vows equality of men and women. One non-traditional wedding vow reads as follows :

> " The sun smiles on us today, our wedding day, and how can it not, for our love is stronger than forever and our hearts beat together as one. My joy is indescribable as I take you as my husband/wife this day and promise to be a true and faithful husband/wife from this day forward, in all life's circumstances, as we face them together. In the joys and sorrows, the good times , and bad, in sickness or in health, I

will always be there for you, to comfort you, love you, honour and cherish you, now and forever".

For a compilation of wedding vows popular under different Christian faiths, see Diane Warner, *Complete Book of Wedding Vows*, Career Press, New Jersy, USA, 1966.
Following the marriage vows, the minister asks for blessing of the rings :

"Bless, O Lord, by which this man and this woman have bound themselves to each other, through Jesus Christ our Lord. Amen."

Then the bride and groom exchange their rings. This completes the marriage ceremony. The minister then joins the right hands of the bride and groom, and pronounces them husband and wife with the following words :

" I pronounce that you are husband and wife, in the name of the father, and the Son, and of the Holy Spirit. Those whom God has joined together let no one put asunder".
The groom is then asked to kiss the bride.
At the end of the wedding ceremony, the bride throws a bouquet of flowers in the air and the girl who catches it is likely to be the one to get married next.

Wedding Vows of Queen Elizabeth II

It might be of some interest to see the wedding vows taken by the British Queen Elizabeth II as an example of the Protestant wedding vows taken by the British Royalty in our times. This is presented in the Appendix. Although the wording has changed here and there, the expression of sentiments and thoughts over centuries in royal weddings has remained virtually unchanged. The present author is grateful to the Buckingham Palace and the archivist of the palace for providing the relevant documents.

10.6 Roman Catholic Wedding

According to the Roman Catholic tradition, marriage is an indissoluble sacrament. The Roman Catholic Church has also discouraged its people from marrying people who are not Catholics. Their belief is that mixed marriages interrupt the process of passing on the faith to the next generation. To obtain approval for interfaith weddings, the Catholic partner must promise that the children resulting from the marriage will be baptized and raised as Catholics. In the Catholic tradition, only the authority of the Pope or his representative can grant the annulment of a marriage.

The Roman Catholic wedding ceremony differs from the Protestant only in some small details. The bride and the groom each carry lighted candles denoting the Light of the Lord. The bride and groom often are asked to sip wine from the same goblet.

10.7 The Indian Christians

The Indian Christians are concentrated in the State of Kerala, and in the north-eastern states of Mizoram and Nagaland, which had been under effective missionary influence. They are also found in large numbers in Goa, Calcutta and Bombay.

St Thomas the Apostle is said to have arrived in India in 54 A.D. Later, with the advent of the Portugese, the French and the British in India, there was further Christian influence.

In India, Christians are basically converts, although there are descendants of European settlers and Anglo-Indians. Many of them had been converted to Christianity to escape the rigidity of the Hindu caste system. On the positive side, the charitable work of the British missionaries in India appealed to the Hindus who occupied low position in the social and economic scales.

A small segment of the Indian Christians are known as Anglo-Indians, that is, Indians of the British origin. They are descendants of British men, generally from the colonial service and the military, and lower-caste Hindu or Muslim women. Both the British and the

Indian societies rejected the offspring of these unions, and so the Anglo-Indians, as they became known, sought marriage partners among other Anglo-Indians.

10.8 The Indian Christian Wedding Ceremony

The Indian Christian wedding ceremony largely follows the Protestant wedding ceremony. However, some traditional local customs have become a part of the ceremony. For some details on the influence of Hindu customs on Christian marriages in India, see T.N. Verghese, " An Examination of the Influence of Hindu Customs and Manners on the Christians of Kerala", Unpublished M.A. Dissertation, Perkins School of Theology, Southern Methodist University, Texas, 1974.

- A prayer is said in the respective houses of the bride and the groom before they proceed to the church in a procession.
- The bride in her wedding veil is accompanied by a couple of girls holding flower baskets. The groom comes along with his "bestman". Trumpets are blown, presumably to ward off evil spirits.
- The bride and the groom are not expected to see one another on the wedding day until they stand together to exchange marriage vows and exchange wedding rings.
- The officiating minister asks the couple to hold one another's hand. They take the oath of loyalty to one another. Then the priest declares them " Man and Wife" and they are asked to exchange rings.
- Eye witnesses say that in addition to exchanging rings, they also exchange flower garlands and exchange lighted candles.

The gathering sprinkles rice upon the couple. It is a symbolic gesture of wishing the newly married couple fertility, as is common in the Western Christian wedding ceremonies.

10.9 Women in Christianity

This section provides a brief overview of the status of women in Christianity.

All religions agree that women should be treated properly, not abused or mistreated. Some religions argue that their norms represent an improvement in the treatment over what their predecessors did. But "none of the major world religions---Judaism, Christianity, Islam, Buddhism, Hinduism---treat women equally, though they fail to a greater or lesser extent" (Rita M. Ross, *Feminism and Religion*). The difference is one of degree. Most religious fundamentalists contend that the religious texts are revealed. Even though these scriptures grew out of a male-dominated patriarchal social structure, they are believed by the Christian fundamentalists to be timeless and largely unalterable.

Following the same approach as adopted in the discussion of other religious traditions, this section provides a glimpse of the familial and social position of women as reflected in the Christian tradition. The scope is limited to the main body of the Christian scriptures, the New Testament of the Bible. Needless to say, it does not portray the position of women of Christian faith in the world of today.

Many interpreters of the Bible and especially the feminist scholars find numerous examples in the New Testament to suggest that Christian women occupy an inferior position to men in the family unit and in the society at large.

- Man and Woman Created Unequal

The story of Genesis in the Bible states that God created man in His own image and God is conceived as gender-specific. "Then the Lord God made a woman from the rib He had taken out of this man.' (Genesis 2, 22-24). Many feminists see in this the roots of gender inequality.

- Wife Subjugated to Husband

There are numerous passages that are quoted by feminist scholars which exhort wives to be subject to their husbands.

"Wives, be subject to your own husbands, as to the Lord. For the husband is the head of the wife, as Christ also is head of the Church......But as the Church is subject to Christ, so also the wives ought to be to their husbands in everything." (*Ephesians* 5:22-24)

A close parallel is found in *Colossians* in which Paul writes :

"And whatever you do in word or deed, do all in the name of the Lord Jesus, giving thanks through Him to God the Father. Wives, be subject to your husbands, as is fitting in the Lord." (*Colossians* (3:17-18))

In his first first letter to Corinth, Paul emphasized that the married Christian woman should be devoted to pleasing her husband, a duty overshadowed only by her allegiance to the will of god where the two might be in conflict(*Corinthians* 7:34)

- Wives Subordinate in Social and Spiritual Role

Several passages in the Bible have also been quoted to suggest that wives should allow their husbands to play the role of leadership, both in the social aspects of marriage and in the spiritual guidance of the home.

For instance,
"Let the woman learn in quietness with all subjection. For Adam was first formed, then Eve. And Adam was not deceived, but the woman being deceived was in transgression."((I *Timothy* 2:11b, 13-14))

Another passage, ascribed to Peter, closely parallels the Pauline doctrine.

> " In the same way, you wives, be submissive to your own husbands so that even if any of them are disobedient to the word, they may be won without a word by the behaviour of their wives." (*Peter* 3:1))

Another passage states :

> " Let the women keep silent in the churches ; for they are not permitted to speak, but let them subject themselves, just as the Law also says. And if they desire to learn anything, let them ask their own husbands at home ; for it is improper for a woman to speak in the church." (*Corinthians* (14:33-35))

Another passage in the Bible states :

> "Let a woman quietly receive instruction with entire submissiveness. But I do not allow a woman to teach or exercise authority over a man, but to remain quiet." (*Timothy* (2:11-12))

Ordination of women in the Christian church has continued to be a major issue until this day.

- Woman and Motherhood

The Bible, like the scriptures of other religions---Judaism, Islam, and Hinduism pay a glowing tribute to the woman's unique role in bearing children and making possible the survival of human race.
One of the passages (I *Timothy* 2:15) has been interpreted in the following ways (for details see Lesley F. Massey, *Woman and the New Testament*, 1989) :

First, in spite of woman's foolish deception which brought sin into the world through Eve, woman became the essential instrument for producing the Savior, specifically the childbearing of Mary.

Second, childbearing, including the rearing and instruction of children and keeping of the home, is the highest ideal in Christian womanhood and is the lifestyle by which a Christian wife attains eternal life.

- New Testament and Woman's Code of Conduct

The Bible prescribes a code of conduct for a good and faithful Christian wife. A few of these are mentioned below :

1. She must be a good wife in subjugation to her husband (Ephesians 5: 22)
2. She must be a good mother to her children (Titus 2:4)
3. She must avoid the temptation of gossip, slander, and backbiting (I Timothy 5:13)
4. She must be modest and discreet in dress (I Peter 3 : 3-4)

For a more detailed discussion of the issues and assessment of the position of women in the Christian scriptures and tradition, see

- Lesly F. Massey, *Women and the New Testament*, Mcfarland and Co., 1989.
- Arvind Sharma and Katherine Young (Eds.), *Her Voice, Her Faith*, Westview, 2003.
- Rita M. Gross, *Feminism and Religion*, Beacon Press, 1996.

Chapter 11

Jewish Marriage

11.1 Background And Founding of Judaism

- The Jewish religion or Judaism, as it is more popularly
  known, is one of the two oldest religions of the world (the
  other being Hinduism). It is believed to be about 4,000 years
  old.

- Because of their troubled history, Jewish people are scattered
  around the world. The total world population of the Jewish
  faith is estimated to be of the order of 15 million. About 40
  % live in Israel, 45% in USA, and the rest are small
  minorities in other nations [for source of information, see
  MN-30]. There are 350,000 Jews in Canada. Other countries
  which have more than 250,000 Jews are France (600,000),
  Russia (550,000), UK (300,0000), and Argentina (250,000).

- The Jewish religion is monotheistic. The Jewish people
  believe that God revealed himself to Abraham and is the
  creator and the sole ruler of the universe.

- The first five books of the Bible, The Old Testament,
  constitute the *Torah*. Torah, along with a large amount of
  sermonic literature from other sources with commentaries
  and oral traditions constitute the *Talmud* (edited during the 5th
  Century). The Talmud deals with every area of Jewish life,
  including rituals for worship and prayers, marriage customs,
  duties of the husband and wife, food, family life, community
  festivals---all reflecting obedience to the laws of God. Several
  parts of the Talmud are comparable to the Laws of Manu of
  the Hindu scripture. The Torah, which includes the Ten
  Commandments that Moses received from God on Mount
  Sinai, constitutes the guiding principles for the devoutly
  Jewish.

- Jews are expected to observe *Sabbath* (Friday sundown and Saturday night are specially earmarked for worship and rest from labor).
- Jews, like the Muslims, are prohibited to eat pork and camel meat and are expected to eat only animals that are ceremonially slaughtered ('Kosher' meat). See MN-31 for more on Jewish dietary laws.
- Jews believe that the Messiah, savior of humanity, is yet to come.
- Persecution of the Jews and mourning the destruction of the Second Holy Temple in Jerusalem by the Romans (70 C.E.) are mirrored in the Jewish wedding ceremony (see below).

Instead of footnotes, some details are placed at the end of the book under the title " Miscellaneous Notes" (MN---numbered).

11.2 Jews of India

The most important Jewish peoples of India are the Bene Israel, whose main population centers were and still are Cochin, Bombay, Calcutta, Delhi, Goa, and Ahmedabad. There are about 100,000 Jews who report Judaism as their religious faith (see World Jewish Congress, *The Jewish Population of the World*, Lerner Publication Company, 1998).

The native language of the Bene Israel is Marathi. They resemble the non-Jewish Maratha people in appearance and customs, which indicates intermarriage between Jews and native Indians. However, the Bene Israel maintained the practices of Jewish dietary laws, circumcision, and observance of Sabbath as a day of rest.

The three other Jewish groups are Cochin Jews from North Africa, the Sephardic Jews from Europe, and the "Baghdadis" from Iraq and other parts of Middle East. Each group practiced important elements of Judaism and had active synagogues.

The Bene Israel ("Sons of Israel") claim to be descendents of Jews who escaped persecution in Galilee in the 2nd century BCE. Other

Jewish groups put the arrival of their ancestors in India at the time of the Assyrian exile in 722 B.C.E., the Babylonian exile in 586 and after the destruction of the Second Temple in 70 CE.

The Bible contains the first mention of Jews and their connection with India. The Book of Esther, which dates from the second century B.C.E., cites decrees enacted by Ahasuerus relating to the Jews dispersed throughout the provinces of his empire from Hodu to Kush. Hodu is Hebrew for India; and Kush is Ethiopia.

Talmudic and Midrashic literature also mention spices, perfumes, plants, animals, textiles, gems and crockery which bear names of Indian origin.

The earliest documentation of permanent Jewish settlements in India consists of two copper plates now stored in Cochin's main synagogue.

Engraved in the ancient Tamil language, they detail the privileges granted to a certain Joseph Rabban by Bhaskara Ravi Varma, the fourth-century Hindu ruler of Malabar.

There are many old and beautiful synagogues in Cochin and Bombay bearing the ancestry of the Jewish settlements.

The Jews have adopted many of their host country's customs. The Jewish community prospered during the British times and developed important trading links with the Middle East and Europe. Although numerically a small community, they gradually moved into professional categories and still occupy important positions in the civil service and especially in the army.

For more historical details of Jewish settlements in India, see Nathan Katz, *Who Are the Jews of India?* University of California Press, November 2000.

11.3 Jewish Marriage Customs : Evolution

Marriage customs and the form of the wedding ceremony, and the ideal nature of the marital relationship are all laid down in the Talmud.

Concept of Marriage

Marriage in the Jewish tradition is considered to be a religious duty. In the Hebrew language, betrothal is called *kiddushin*, which literally means "sanctification". It is emphasized in Jewish scriptures that marrying is fulfilling a spiritual mission and it enriches family life. Procreation is stressed as an important purpose of marriage so that Jewish values can be transmitted to the next generation. Population growth is stressed as essential for survival of the Jewish people.

Groom Dowry

In Biblical times purchasing the bride was the only way a man could get married. More appropriately, a young man's father had to buy a bride for his son through financial negotiations and by entering into a contract with the bride's father. Thus the dowry system was a part of the matrimonial relationship.

Some Jewish scholars have tried to explain this practice in the following manner. In an agrarian society, young girls like boys were breadwinners as they worked on farms; they worked as shepherd-girls in the fields, and also helped in the kitchen. After the marriage, the bride moved to the groom's house and lived with his parents' house providing a helping hand in way as she had done in her father's household. It was considered fair that the groom's father was to compensate the bride's family. This compensation was to be in the form of a dowry (*mohar*) .

After the dowry was settled, betrothal (*Kiddushin*, which literally means sanctified) was announced in a ceremony. But the bride continued to live in her father's house for at least one year. Some Jewish historians think this was a kind of testing period—a cooling off period in modern terminology. Either side could break off the betrothal if either side changed its mind.

When the two sides were ready to solemnize the marriage, the bride and the groom were led by their respective parties of relatives and friends to the marriage canopy—since ancient times referred to as *Chuppah*.

Thus betrothal and marriage ceremonies remained two distinct events from the Biblical times to the Middle Ages. In later periods, the mohar paid was not considered to be a purchase price of the bride, but rather a gift from the groom's family to the new bride.

By the twelfth century, betrothal and wedding began to disappear as distinct ceremonies separated by several years. The Jewish scholars speculate on two reasons for this. First, for relatively poor families holding two ceremonies with lavish feasts was much too expensive. Second, since the future of Jews was far from certain from year to year, and they often had to flee from one place to another they wanted to eliminate such a long gap in time.

Before the betrothal and wedding ceremonies were merged, even though the betrothal was a serious form of agreement, it was only verbal and had no legal force. After the merger of the two ceremonies, the conditions were put in writing. Ashkenazim Jews developed standard forms for this during the twelfth century. Ashkenazic Jews are the Jews of France, Germany, and Eastern Europe. Sephardic Jews are the Jews of Spain, Portugal, North Africa and the Middle East. The word "Ashkenazic" is derived from the Hebrew word for Germany. The word "Sephardic" is derived from the Hebrew word for Spain.

A ceremony developed during which the agreement was read and signed. This document was called *Tenaim* and was a condition for what would today be called the first condition for engagement.

At the end of the marriage ceremony, the bride and the bridegroom signed the marriage contract (*ketubah*) in the presence of witnesses. The ketubah delineated the fundamental responsibilities undertaken by the husband, and included a part stating how the property is to be divided in case of divorce.

The site of the wedding ceremony has undergone changes over the centuries.

Old Jewish literature and folklore indicate that in Biblical times the ceremony was held outdoors on the premises of the groom's family. By the fifteenth century, the marriage ceremony would occasionally take place in the synagogue.

Auspicious Days

Throughout the ages, certain days have been considered to be auspicious and others to be avoided for a wedding ceremony.

- Tuesday has traditionally been considered a lucky day for Jewish weddings. A Jewish writer who lived in Jerusalem wrote, "….On afternoons on a Tuesday in Jerusalem so many brides, grooms, and photographers flock to the Western Wall that one wonders if any single men and women remain in the town."
- Friday is frequently the wedding day because the Shabbat meal could also be the wedding feast.
- Sunday is not a customary day for weddings, because no preparation could be made on Shabbat. But it has become a very popular day for wedding in the Western world.
- According to the ancient Jewish calendar, the month of June is a traditional time for expression of sorrows and is prohibited for celebration of a joyous occasion like wedding.

For details, see Donna Berman et al, *When a Jew Celebrates*, Berman House Inc., N.J. (1971).

Arranged Marriage

In the traditional Jewish community, intermarriages between Jew and Non-Jews are discouraged but with the change of time and social environment, this is changing.

Until very recently, parents were responsible for arranging marriages of their children. Either the father or the professional matchmaker (*shadkhan*) arranged the match. For a long time matchmaking was a highly respected vocation. Often Jewish clergy (*Rabbis*) used to perform the function of matchmaking. For his services, the rabbi used to get a percentage of the dowry.

The use of services of a professional matchmaker is not as widespread as it was in olden days. But, as we all know, the Jewish population is widely scattered across the world. In spite of easier and frequent meeting between young adult boys and girls, it is not uncommon to see the use of professional matchmaker's services even today.

The majority of Jewish marriages in India are still arranged. The traditional groom-dowry is observed in a ceremonial form. The bridal-dowry where the bride's father pays a dowry to the groom has become more common, following other communities in India. Indian Jewish women now wear bindis, the small marks in the middle of their foreheads that at one time signified a woman's marital status but are now a part of cosmetic and fashion.

Prohibited Marriages

The Torah sets forth a list of prohibited relations. Such marriages are never valid in the eyes of the Jewish law. A man cannot marry certain close blood relatives, the ex-wives of certain close blood relatives, a woman who has not been validly divorced from her previous husband, the daughter or granddaughter of his ex-wife, or the sister of his ex-wife during the ex-wife's lifetime. The offsprings of such marriages are bastards and illegitimate (*mamzerim*), and are subject to a variety of restrictions. However, it is important to note that only the offspring of these incestuous or forbidden marriages are mamzerim. Children born out of wedlock are not mamzerim in Jewish law and bear no stigma.

There are other classes of marriages that are not permitted. The marriage of minors, and of a Jew to a non-Jew fall into this category.

11.4 Jewish Wedding Ceremony

Jewish wedding customs and traditions bear a close resemblance to those in the other oldest religion, Hinduism.

- The Jewish wedding ceremony is quite elaborate like the traditional Hindu wedding ceremony. Most Jewish families try to follow the traditional customs to the letter.
- As already mentioned, as in a Hindu marriage, a Jewish wedding is sanctified on certain auspicious days.

- Both the bride and the groom are expected to remain on fast on the wedding day until the ceremony has been completed.
- It seems that the number seven is very auspicious in the Jewish tradition as it is the Hindu tradition. Possibly for a different reason, but as described below, the bride circles the 'chuppah' seven times.
  Also, seven blessings are recited in a traditional Jewish wedding ceremony, as described below.

The following are the steps in a traditional Jewish marriage including the pre-wedding ceremony.

Vort (Engagement Ceremony)

After the boy and the girl along with the two families have decided to go ahead with the wedding, they usually make a formal announcement in a special gathering (called 'Vort') sometime before the actual wedding. 'Vort', in Hebrew language means 'word' as in giving one's word. Most families sign a contract, the *tenaim,* meaning "conditions," that lays down the obligations of each side regarding the wedding, and a final date for the wedding is agreed upon. According to the Jewish tradition, one week before the wedding the groom and bride, the *chatan* and *kallah* respectively, stop seeing each other, in order to enhance the joy of their wedding through their separation.

Ufruf (Pre-Wedding Ceremony)

On the Shabbat of the week before the wedding, the groom (*Chatan*) is called to the altar to recite the blessings from the Torah. It is meant to impress upon the groom the duty to look to the Torah as guide in married life. The congregation showers him with raisins and nuts, symbolic of their wishes for a sweet and fruitful marriage blessed with many children.

On the same Shabbat, the bride's (*Kallah*) family and friends arrange a similar gathering party for her, expressing the same wishes for her. It is called Shabat Kallah.

Fasting

According to traditional Jewish custom, the bride as well as the groom remain on fast for the whole day until after the ceremony. Since each is starting life anew, fasting takes on the character of a Day of Atonement (*Yom Kippur*), when all wrongs are forgiven and the couple can start married life with a clean slate. This, as discussed elsewhere, fasting by the couple as well as the bestower of the bride is also mandatory under the Hindu custom, probably for a different reason.

Presence of a Rabbi

Since marriage under the Jewish law is essentially a private contractual agreement between a man and a woman, the presence of a Rabbi is not mandatory. It is common, however, for Rabbis to officiate, partly in imitation of the Christian practice and partly because the presence of a religious or civil official is required under the civil law in many countries. This practice has been adopted in other parts of the world, including India.

Ketubah (Marriage Contract)

As part of the wedding ceremony, the husband gives the wife a *ketubah*. The ketubah refers to the marriage contract which is prepared before the wedding and is read aloud. The *ketubah,* written in Aramaic, is ordained by Talmudic law and according to some scholars dates back to Biblical times.

In olden days the Ketubah used to spell out the husband's obligations to the wife during marriage, conditions of inheritance upon his death, and obligations regarding the support of children of the marriage. It also provided for the wife's support in the event of divorce.

The ketubah has much in common with prenuptial agreements. Initially, such agreements were historically disfavored, because it was thought that anticipating divorce would encourage divorce, and that people who considered the possibility of divorce should not be marrying in the first place. Many Rabbis, however, maintain that a ketubah discouraged divorce, by serving as a constant reminder of the husband's substantial financial obligations if he divorced his wife. Sometimes a Ketubah is exquisitely calligraphed and decorated with colorful Jewish motifs (see an illustration of a modern day Ketubah in the Appendix).

Bedekin (Veiling the Bride)

After the signing of the *ketubah,* which is usually accompanied by refreshment, groom does the *bedekin,* or "veiling". The groom, together with his father and future father-in-law, is accompanied by musicians and the male guests to the room where the bride is receiving her guests. She is veiled. She sits, like a queen, on a throne-like chair surrounded by her family and friends. The groom, who has not seen her for a week, uncovers her face. This ceremony is mainly for the legal purpose of the groom identifying the bride before the wedding.

It is not exactly known since when this became a common practice. It is interesting to note in this context that there is a Biblical story (as described in the chapter on Christian marriage) that Jacob was in love with Laban's younger daughter, Rachel. But Laban tricked into marrying his elder daughter, Leah, with Jacob. As Leah was covered with a veil, Jacob was unable to see that he was getting married to Leah instead of Rachel.

Chuppah (Canopy)

The next stage is known as the *chuppah* (sometime also called *huppa)*, or "canopy." Chuppah is a kind of large canopy consisting of four posts held securely to the floor. This ceremonial canopy is beautifully decorated with flowers and colorful fabric. The chuppah is symbolic of the making of a new home for the couple.

It is usually held outside, under the stars, as a sign of the blessing given by God to the patriarch Abraham, that his children shall be "as the stars of the heavens." The groom is accompanied to the 'chuppah' by his parents, and usually wears a white robe, known as a *kittel,* to indicate the fact that for the bride and groom, life is starting anew with a clean white slate, since they are uniting to become a new entity, without past sins.

The bride and groom usually fast on the day of the wedding (until the *chuppah* ceremony) since for them it is like *Yom Kippur,* the Day of Atonement.

When the bride arrives at the *chuppah* she circles the groom seven times with her mother and future mother-in-law, while the groom continues to pray. According to Jewish scholars, this symbolizes the idea of the woman being a protective force for the new household from the evil eyes.

The number seven parallels the seven days of creation, and symbolizes the fact that the bride and groom are about to create their own "new world" together.

The bride, bridegroom, rabbi, and two witnesses stand beneath the chuppah. The bride and groom groom face Israel and in Israel, they stand facing Jerusalem.
The girl's father offers the hands of the bride to the groom. After citing the date of the year (counted from the Creation), the month and day of the week, and the persons in the contract, the bridegroom states :

> "Be unto me a wife according to the Law of Moses and Israel, and I, according to the word of God, will worship, honour, maintain, and govern thee according to the manner of husbands among the Jews, which do worship, honour, maintain, and govern their wives faithfully; I also do bestow on thee the dower of thy virginity---which belongs to thee by law, and moreover, thy food, thy apparel, and sufficient necessaries."

Kiddushin (The Ring)

The groom, now takes a plain gold ring and places it on the finger of the bride, and recites in the presence of two witnesses,

> "Behold you are sanctified (betrothed) to me with this ring, according to the Law of Moses and Israel."

He places a ring on her finger. In the Western society the wedding ring is worn on the third finger of the left hand. But in the Jewish tradition, the ring is placed on the index finger of the *right* hand of the bride.
The *ketuvah* is now read aloud, usually by another honoree, after which it is given to the bride.

commonly found among the people of Assam in India. He is expected to break it with his feet to show his masculine power. If he is unable to do that, he has to please the bridemaids by giving gifts to earn his way to the wedding court.

For more details on the Jewish customs including wedding ceremonies and their significance, see Leo Trepp, *Judaism : Development and Life* (1966), and Donna Berman et al, *When a Jew Celebrates*, Berman House Inc., N.J. (1971).

Celebration

In Jewish tradition, weddings have been considered to be an occasion for elaborate and extensive celebrations. In Genesis (29:22) Laban "gathered together all the men of the place", and made a feast to celebrate his giving Leah to Jacob and Biblical scholars speak of a week-long celebration following a wedding in which one day was reserved for feeding the poor.

Judaism and Divorce

Judaism recognized the concept of "no-fault" divorce thousands of years ago. Judaism has always accepted divorce as a fact of life, albeit an unfortunate one. Judaism generally maintains that it is better for a couple to divorce than to remain together in a state of constant bitterness and strife.

Jewish scholars point out that this does not mean that Judaism takes divorce lightly. Many aspects of Jewish law discourage divorce. The procedural details involved in arranging a divorce are complex and exacting. Except in certain cases of misconduct by the wife, a man who divorces his wife is required to pay her substantial sums of money, as specified in the ketubah (marriage contract). In addition, Jewish law prohibits a man from remarrying his ex-wife after she has married another man.

Sheva Berakhot (The Seven Blessings)

After this, the *Sheva Berakhot,* or seven blessings, are recited by t
officiating Rabbi. These blessings are also recited over a full cup
wine. The blessings begin with praising God for His creation in
general and creation of the human being and proceed with praise
the creation of the human as a "two part creature," woman and m
The blessings express the hope that the new couple will rejoice
together forever as though they are the original couple, Adam and
Eve in the Garden of Eden. The blessings also include a prayer tha
Jerusalem will be fully rebuilt and restored with the Temple in its
midst and the Jewish people within her gates.

Mazel Tove (Breaking the Wine Glass)

At the conclusion of the blessings, after the couple drinks from the
second cup, the groom breaks the glass with his foot. The assembly
cries out :
"Mazel Tove, Mazel Tove" (Good Luck, Good Luck !)

Many Jewish scholars of antiquity believe that in the midst of
rejoicing it is a reminder of the destruction of the Second Holy
Jewish Temple by the Romans (70 C.E.). It is a reminder that the
Jewish nation is as shattered as the pieces of a shattered wine glass
and it is a spiritual pledge for the couple to work as life partners
toward unifying the Jewish people of the world.
In Indian Jewish wedding ceremonies, a slight variation of this
custom has been reported. They put ashes on the foreheads of the
bride and groom as a sad reminder of the burning of their homes and
exile in a foreign land. It also signifies hope for a new home.
Smashing various kinds of pottery before or after wedding was a
common ritual in the ancient world. Curiously enough the customs
of breaking a betel nut and also smashing a plate made of clay are
found in some Hindu wedding ceremonies in India. Interpretations
differ, however. Before the groom is escorted to the wedding court, a
betel nut is placed in front of him by the bride's friends. This is

11.5 Women in Judaism

Consistent with the approach to include an assessment of the position of women in other religions discussed in this book, the focus is on the Jewish scriptures and not on the actual status in modern times. The old Jewish tradition, customs, and laws of marriage and divorce reflected the bias of a male dominated patriarchal social structure. One scholar has summed up in the following words,

> " ...in the formative period of Judaism, the status of women was not one of equality with men, but rather, severe inferiority. Since the sacred and secular spheres of that society were intertwined, this inferiority and subordination of women are consequently present in both the religious and civil areas of Jewish life" (Leonard Swidler, *Women in Judaism*, 1976).

Jewish and non-Jewish scholars including several feminists quote many instances from the Jewish scriptures to support the above conclusion. A few of these are reproduced below:

- In a wedding ceremony or any community festival or prayer at a synagogue, ten Jewish men are considered as the required quorum (*minyan*). Women are not counted toward this quorum.
- The only way Jews could survive as Jews in exile was by learning the Jewish laws and scriptures and practicing them in the real world. Jewish women were excluded from several religious activities that involved rituals. Some Rabbinical interpretations of the Torah even went so far as to imply that women were prohibited to read or recite Torah---the sacred laws of the Jewish.
- According to the Torah and the Talmud, a man was permitted to marry more than one wife (polygamy), but a woman could not marry more than one man (polyandry) . Around 1000 C.E., Ashkenazic Jewry (reformed) banned

polygamy because of pressure from the predominant Christian culture. To the present day, Yemenite and Ethiopian Jews continue to practice polygamy; however, the modern State of Israel allows only one wife, unless you come to Israel with more than one wife, in which case you can keep the wives you have but you cannot marry new ones.

- The position of husband and wife with regard to divorce is not an equal one. According to the Talmud, only the husband can initiate a divorce, and the wife cannot prevent him from divorcing her. Under Jewish law, a man can divorce a woman for any reason. The Talmud specifically says that a man can divorce a woman simply because he finds another woman more attractive by paying her the ketubah, and the woman's consent to the divorce is not required. In fact Jewish law requires divorce in some circumstances: when the wife commits a sexual transgression, a man must divorce her, even if he is inclined to forgive her.

Later rabbinical authorities took steps to ease the harshness of these rules by prohibiting a man from divorcing a woman without her consent. In addition, a rabbinical court can compel a husband to divorce his wife under certain circumstances: when he is physically repulsive because of some medical condition or when he violates or neglects his marital obligations (food, clothing and sexual relation), or, according to some views, when there is sexual incompatibility. Some liberal sections of the Rabbis have supported the move to change some of the harsh and unjust Jewish laws and yet retain the core Jewish values. For instance, under Jewish law, only the man can initiate divorce; thus, if the husband cannot be found, she cannot obtain a divorce and she cannot marry another man. If she does, she would be regarded as *augean* (a transgression that would affect the status of offspring of the marriage). To prevent this problem, it is customary in many places for a man to give his wife a conditional divorce before he goes to war.

Chapter 12

Marriages In Tribal Society

Tribal societies in all parts of the world still maintain some distinctive characteristics of the ancient way of life and culture including marriage customs. However, with increased contacts and interaction with the mainstream civilization, aided by improved means of transportation and communication, the distinctive identity of such cultures is slowly disappearing. From time to time, many anthropologists and sociologists have conducted research on their changing ways of life and culture. A detailed discussion of marriage customs in tribal societies in a global context is beyond the scope of the present book. For a detailed discussion of many original marriage customs in tribal societies in some geographic regions, see Will Durant, *The Story of Civilization*, Vol. I, 1954.

This chapter focuses on some marriage customs and ceremonies still prevalent among some of the major tribes of India.

12.1 Tribals of India

The tribal or aboriginal ('Adivasis') society of India follows a wide variety of marriage customs and practices. Sometimes the customs followed by the tribal people are similar to those of other religions but quite often they have been given the legal right to practice that are somewhat unique to their own age-old traditions.

The tribal population accounts for about 7 percent of the total population of India. Some of the major tribes live in Madhya Pradesh (Bhil,Oraon, Khond, Munda, Baiga), West Bengal, Orissa, and Bihar (Santal, Munda), Andhra Pradesh (Gond), Tamil Nadu (Sholagar, Urali).

Their Religion

The tribal people practice a variety of religious faiths including some forms of Hinduism, Islam, Christianity and a mixture of Nature worship and animism.

Instead of footnotes, some details are placed at the end of the book under the title " Miscellaneous Notes" (MN---numbered).

12.2 Some Tribal Marriage Customs

Exogamy

Exogamy is strictly practiced in most tribal communities with minor exceptions. Marriages and extramarital sexual relations between a man and woman within the same clan are considered as incestuous and are penalized by the community chiefs. Sometimes fines are imposed. For instance, among the Bhantus, fines are imposed in the form of paying for a feast where the man and woman have to undergo a ceremonial bath as a process of purification of their bodies.

There are three exogamous groups :
- A man is not allowed to marry a girl of the same village . This means that the bride must be from a different village.
- A man must not marry a woman who belongs to a group worshipping the same number of gods. This means that a clan worshipping seven gods are prohibited from marrying a woman belonging to the clan worshipping seven gods.
- A man belonging to the same 'totem' must marry a woman belonging to a different totem . A totem is a guardian spirit, an animal or plant from which members of the group claim descent or kinship. Groups which have the same totem cannot intermarry.

Some sociologists and anthropologists trace the widespread popularity and strict adherence to exogamy to the hostage theory , a relic of the old concept of taking in a wife from a hostile group (marriage by capture).

Since marriage by capture is prohibited by law, the tribal communities follow an ingenious practice. After the marriage has been negotiated and a ceremony has been conducted, a mock marriage by capture is enacted to preserve their tradition. For instance, Gonds in Madhya Pradesh and Muthuvans of South India enter into a mock fight and capture the bride. A more modern form of marrying outside the clan is exchange of daughters. When a man marries a woman outside his clan, the family gives another woman from the family to the bride's clan in marriage. This is marriage by exchange. This means replacement of an asset concerned with the reproductive capacity so necessary for continuity of the group.

Groom-Dowry

Groom-Dowry, a dowry paid by the groom or bride price, is very common among most tribal communities. In many Adivasi communities the bride price is commuted by means of service rendered by the bridegroom (e.g., the Bhils of Madhya Pradesh). The groom-dowry is given to the bride's father and she does not receive any share of it, unlike the Mahr in Muslim marriage. The amount of groom-dowry is a matter of pride for the bride as it is taken to be a measure of her desirability.

Polygamy and and Polyandry

Among the Indian tribes, two types of polyandry are in vogue. When several brothers share the same wife, as among the Khasas and Todas, it is known as 'fraternal polyandry'.

In some tribes when the eldest brother marries a girl, she automatically becomes the common wife of all adult brothers. This is common where the male population is small relative to females. On the other hand, polygamy (one husband marrying many brides) is common among the Naga tribes, the Gond, the Baigas where women outnumber men.

Bow and Arrow Ceremony

In some tribes, a ceremony is held where all brothers and the common wife assemble amidst the rest of the villagers in the fourth month of pregnancy of the wife. As a result of consensus, one of the brothers presents a set of bow and arrow to the wife. This is taken as a declaration that he will be accepted as the father of the coming child.

Pre-marital and Extra-marital Sex

Pre-marital sex relations are tolerated or permitted in varying degrees in the tribal community so long as they do not lead to pregnancy. If pregnancy occurs, the girl is asked to declare the father in the tribal assembly and he is forced to marry her. Extra-marital relations are less common than pre-marital relations. Since the tribal marriages are not a religious sacrament, dissolution of a marriage is granted legally and easily if the parties no longer wish to live together.

Ghotuls

In many tribals regions (e.g., Madhya Pradesh), there are Ghotuls. Ghotuls are co-educational dormitories where both young boys and girls can spend time together and even live together. Equality, simplicity, and freedom form the fundamental fabric of the Ghotul life. These dormitories are expected to prepare young boys and girls to select their life partners and learn about the duties and responsibilities of married life through free intermixing. Because of their sexual freedom, at the time of marriage, neither is the bride a virgin, nor is the groom inexperienced.
Members eat, play, and sleep without any separation of males and females. They can even swim in the river together without clothes on. There are, however, some rules that must be obeyed and some disciplines must be observed. The local tribal councils enforce these

rules. For instance, if a girl becomes pregnant she must assign responsibility for the pregnancy. The elders of the tribal community negotiate a marriage in such cases of accidental pregnancy and the husband must take full responsibility for the child.

12.3 Tribal Wedding Ceremonies

Wedding ceremonies of the tribal people are widely different and have their roots in ancient tradition and culture. Community singing and dancing are an essential part of any family or community festival including a wedding ceremony. Even before the children are sent to school, they are taught singing and dancing. *Mahua* is known as the love- tree in many tribal communities. The bride and groom with the ends of their clothes tied circle a Mahua tree. On the wedding day both the bride and the groom drink heavily and dance. All marriage-related and family law matters are first settled at the community level. If not amicably settled, they are handled by local courts which take into account the tribal customs and age-old traditions.

12.4 Miscellaneous Tribal Customs

It is outside the scope of this chapter to go beyond the marriage customs of tribals or aboriginals in India. However, it might be of some interest to note a few common or relatively uncommon customs in other countries.

- Exogamy or marriage outside one's own clan or tribe is more common in the tribal society and owes its origin to marriage by capture in olden days of tribal warfare.
- Even though courtship and free mixing of the sexes is common, extramarital sex is disfavored and often penalties are imposed by the tribal chiefs and chieftains.
- Boys and girls are often free to choose their life partners. But they must obtain the approval of the elders of the local tribe. Unless this is done, the family may be socially ostracized.

- Groom–dowry or bride- price that the groom's family must pay to the bride's father is almost universal in tribal communities. Sociologists say this is a compensation that the groom's family must pay to the bride's family for the loss of a pair working hands. In an agrarian society, women work along with men. Also, giving away a girl means the loss of a reproductive unit for the family and the tribe.

- Dowries are often negotiated and paid in terms of sheep, goats, cows, and agricultural lands. If the groom or the groom's family faces hardship in paying the full dowry, arrangements are made to pay in instalments. Among the Kikuyu tribals who live in Kenya, if the groom's family does not honor its commitment, it would be unable to receive a bride-price when there is a girl to be married.

- It is interesting to note that in some tribal communities there was (and in some communities there is) a kind of same-sex marriage. In the Kikuyu tribe of Kenya, older women would marry the younger women whose husbands have died. The older woman would take care of the young "wife" (she was called a wife). If she has children, their tribal names would be changed to hers. If she does not have children, the "husband" would choose a man for her to have children for her. The young wife would then bear children for her. When the young woman's children reach the age of marriage, the dowry would be paid to the older woman, and if there were sons involved, she would pay the dowry.

The following sources would be found useful for more details :
Baidyanath Saraswati (Ed.), *Tribal Thought and Culture*, 1991.
S.S. Shashi, *Night Life of Indian Tribes*, 1987.
L.P. Vidyarthi, *The Tribal Culture of India*, 1976.

Chapter 13

Women in Hinduism

13.1 Introduction

The social and economic position accorded to women has been a subject of considerable interest in recent decades. In the Christian countries the issue of ordination of women has become a highly controversial issue, and some Churches are facing the prospect of dissension, and even schism, on this question.

This chapter provides a synoptic view of the process of evolution of the role and responsibilities of the husband and wife in family life. It also briefly indicates the changing status of women in general and of the wife in particular in the society.

The present day role and position of women in the Indian social and economic life resemble little to the customs prescribed by the scriptures and the code of ethics and those that were observed in India in the ancient times. Yet, it would serve as an interesting backdrop to the current landscape.

Instead of footnotes, some details are placed at the end of the book under the title " Miscellaneous Notes" (MN---numbered).

The Hindu scriptures and commentaries prescribed in great details the duties and responsibilities of a household including romantic relations between the husband and wife [MN-2]. A detailed discussion of these is beyond the scope of this book. Needless to say, these evolved as part of the contemporary social structure in olden times. They were designed to promote harmony in the family life and social fabric.

Closely interlinked with the process of evolution of these customs and traditions was the changing role and status of women.

Indian culture is at the crossroads. The pattern of economic life, life style, and social customs, along with the status and role of women are changing and changing at a fast pace, thanks to the spread of education, rapid industrialization of the country, expansion of employment opportunities for women with the growth of the service sector, and most importantly, the exposure to the Western values and life styles, aided by the easy access to television and other media. For details, see R.B. Mishra, *Indian Women : Challenges and Change*, Commonwealth Publishers, New Delhi, 1992.

13.2 Women in Ancient India

In several Vedic texts and Upanishads, there are some references to situations and contexts which suggest that women participated in activities and professions that required high levels of education and skills. They enjoyed a highly respected position in society. Some of the texts in Vedas and Upanishads provided that the wife was the half of a man's life and without a married wife a man's life was less than complete [MN-27]. She would accompany and assist her husband in all religious ceremonies and pursuits.

In spite of expressions of reverence for women folk and words glorifying womanhood and motherhood, in the ancient Hindu society, the position of women in general and of the wife in particular was far from being enviable.

According to the present author, the place of respect accorded to and enjoyed by women has been somewhat overdrawn by the Indian social historians.

Especially in post -Vedic periods, there was a definite deterioration in the social status of women and also her place in family life. For instance, the Law of Manu prescribed that her primary duties consisted of procreation and looking after the household. She was expected to have minimum of contacts with men outside the immediate family. The opportunities provided to women for education outside her home were limited. She was expected to be well versed in fine arts only. This is a far cry from the respectable and responsible status that women generally enjoy in the present day India. They play an increasingly active part in the household life, in politics, in government and public administration, in education, in arts and sciences, in business, industry and entrepreneurship. Elsewhere in this book, similar discussions have been provided of the position accorded to women in scriptures of other major religions. Modern-day feminist scholars generally find women to have been accorded a status inferior to men in all living religions including Hinduism. The religious scriptures grew out of a male-dominated social structure and they all reflect in varying degrees gender inequality.

Some scholars have noted, however, that even though "classical Hindu texts give the impression of being immutable, Hindu practices have been fluid and flexible, allowing for adaptations, assimilation, and adjustments" (Arvind Sharma and Katherine Young (eds.), *Her Voice, Her Faith*, 2003).

13.3 Family Structure

The traditional concept of family in the Hindu society and in India at large was a joint (or "an extended") family system. The traditional family unit included parents, brothers, uncles, cousins or nephews who often lived under one roof or a group of roofs. It resembled the early Jewish family structure.

Joint family system made good economic sense as human resources of the family could be pooled for the development of the land. It reduced the need for the division of property. Also, it was a form of economic security in old age.

With industrialization, diversification of employment opportunities, and the need to move to geographic regions away from the ancestral land, the foundation of the traditional joint family system is breaking down. Extensive land reforms that were introduced after independence also played an important role in weakening the joint family structure.

13.4 Child Marriage

It is commonly believed that the Hindu scriptures prescribed child marriage since it has been commonly found in India. There is no suggestion or approval of the child marriage in any of the scriptures or the Hindu Code of Ethics. The husband was expected to be much older than the bride. According to the Law of Manu [MN-15], the ideal marriage was one in which the bride was one third the age of the groom. Thus a man of twenty four should marry a girl of eight. The possible reason for this was a concern for preservation of human race. A younger wife prolonged the reproductive years of married life.

Child marriage was not a religious custom or practice. Yet, it became popular in the Medieval period. The reason for this is not entirely clear---there could be more than one reason.

According to some scholars, "the fear of marauding Muslim invaders encouraged parents to marry their daughters in childhood and confine their wives more strictly in their homes" (A.L. Basham, *The Wonder That Was India*) .

Others point out that the Muslim invasion and forcible abduction of unmarried girls by the invaders probably made it more common but the custom seems to have been prevalent on a limited scale during the pre-Muslim period.

Some others point to the stigma attached to the loss of virginity among the unmarried girls. Once she had lost her virginity, it would be a shame for the family and she would become unmarriageable.

It is still practised, however, in a clandestine manner in remote rural areas. Boys and girls of as young as 7 or 8 have been reported to have been married. This is an illegal practice. Child marriage was prohibited by law in 1929 by the Child Marriages Restraint Act.

13.5 Marriage and Divorce

As already mentioned, according to the Vedas, marriage was a spiritual union and it was a bond that went from birth to birth. Once the seven steps were taken, in principle a marriage was indissoluble. However, later legal texts considered a dissolution under some exceptional circumstances [MN-6]. Provisions relating to divorce usually favoured the man, and the woman was at a disadvantage. Adultery, for instance, was a punishable offence. But the punishment for the wife was more severe than for the husband. The Hindu Marriage Act of 1955 for the first time clearly defined the rights and privileges of women in more equitable terms.

13.6 Widows and Widow Remarriage

For largely unknown and strange reasons, widows were considered as unlucky and inauspicious. They were expected to live a life of austerity, and chastity. Widows were made to believe that it was for the good of her dead husband and for her own good in the next birth. They were kept largely segregated from men who were not members of the same family.

Again, this kind of custom, support for which can be found in the sacred texts, was inequitable and unjust for women. No words are adequate to condemn the insensitive treatment of widows in the Hindu community. A trace of this in milder forms can still be found in many traditional families. In contrast to the Muslim society, in the Hindu tradition there was no provision for widow remarriage. Widow remarriage was not socially acceptable until some 150 years ago. It came to be acceptable due to the efforts of several social reformers [MN-25].

13.7 Women and Education

In the ancient social structure, the primary role of the wife was managing the household and looking after the needs of other family members---a custom practised in most patriarchal forms of society in other religious communities and in other parts of the world. Women's education was considered to be unnecessary. A father's religious duty toward his daughter was thought to be incomplete until he was able to arrange a suitable marriage for the daughter. And this was expected to be done, according to some Hindu code of ethics, before she had attained the age of puberty.

The Muslim invasion and consequent fear of abduction and molesting women encouraged the society to keep the women and especially unmarried girls secluded from the outside. Some scholars point out that during the Muslim rule the Hindus " adopted the system of 'parda', by which from puberty to old age, women were carefully screened from the sight of all men but only their husbands and close relatives"(A.L. Basham, *The Wonder That Was India*). Another writer writes, "In part of India that fell under Muslim domination...Women were barred from social gatherings. They had to accept the veil, a practice that had been totally unknown." (Anwar Hekmat, W*omen and the Koran*, 1997). These changes gradually led to a degeneration in the social and economic status of women over many centuries.

13.8 Women and Property Rights

Women were largely dependent upon men folk for their sustenance and the property rights accorded to women were generally very limited except in segments of Hindu communities which were matrilineal. Some parts of South India were matrilineal. The Hindu Marriage Act of 1955 gave equitable property rights to women in legal and justiceable terms.

Several scholars on religions have emphasized the resilience of the Hindu religion and its ability to be flexible and absorb inevitability of change. As one writer has put it, " Hindus have, over the centuries, been able to keep their tradition vibrant, to interpret sacred texts, and assimilate and adapt practices from the ancient Indus Valley Civilization to the age of the Internet". (Arvind Sharma and Katherine Young (eds.), *Her Voice, Her Faith,* 2003.

For further reading on this chapter, see A.L. Basham (ed.), *A Cultural History of India*, 1975 ; R.C. Majumdar, *Ancient India* , 1952 ; Rita M. Gross, *Feminism and Religion*, 1996 ; and Arvind Sharma and Katherine Young (eds.), *Her Voice, Her Faith*, 2003.

Chapter 14

Some Comparative Customs

14.1 Introduction

Although the outwardly customs and ceremonies were and still are very diverse across countries and religious faiths, there is an underlying thread of unity.There are many elements that make a typical Hindu wedding similar to wedding ceremonies under other faiths. The present author would like to emphasize three such elements.

- One, prayers and benedictions are an essential part of all wedding ceremonies.
- Second, warding off the evil spirits is another element. This is a legacy of the prehistoric times when man was exceedingly dependent upon the elemental forces of Nature.
- Third, as already mentioned, in primitive ages survival of a tribe depended upon its numerical strength and for this reason fertility of women was essential. This is also a legacy of the primitive ages. This explains why some fertility rituals are observed in wedding ceremonies even to this day in many parts of the world and under diverse religious faiths.

Instead of footnotes, some details are placed at the end of the book under the title " Miscellaneous Notes" (MN---numbered).

14.2 Selection of Auspicious Time

In modern Western countries, time to wed is time that is convenient. Weekends are the most convenient and hence most popular. This was not so in olden days. This is not so in the case of marriages in other parts of the world or in types of marriages.

In England, wedding in the month of May was believed to bring bad luck. Queen Victoria declared that she would not allow any of her children to marry in May.

When Mary, Queen of Scots, married the Earl of Bothwell in the month of May, the following line was found affixed to the gates of Holyrood house, Edinburgh on the following morning :

> Mense malum Maio nubere vulgus ait
> (Common folk say 'tis ill to wed in May)

Some chroniclers like Plutarch (C.E. 46- C.E. 125) believed that this prohibition was connected with the Roman May festivals of *Bona Dea,* goddess of chastity, and *lemuralia,* feast of the dead, events which made the month of May inauspicious for wedding [MN-26].

The days of the week were also important. A popular old rhyme goes like this (Margaret Baker, *Wedding Customs and Folklore*, p.56) :

> Monday for wealth,
> Tuesday for health,
> Wednesday best of all,
> Thursday for losses,
> Friday for crosses,
> And Saturday no luck at all.

In most of South Asian countries, the Middle East and Far East including China and Japan, even to this day wedding days are selected by family priests and astrologers.

14. 3 Fertility Rites

In Vedic texts, a typical form of blessing a woman is " Be the mother of a hundred sons". Also many prayers to God ask for children. In modern days, you will be definitely ridiculed if you wished a couple a hundred or even ten children. This was not so in olden days.

Fertility has been at the very center of human survival and happiness. As the Old Testament said,

"God blessed them (Adam and Eve) and said to them, 'Be fruitful and increase in number, fill the earth and subdue it. Rule over the fish of the sea and the birds of the air and over every living creature that moves on the ground." (Genesis, 1, 28)

It is curious to see that some of the customs believed to be associated with fertility are still observed, some quite unconsciously. Throwing of rice or confetti is believed to have been practiced in ancient Roman marriages. In an agrarian society, rice symbolized productivity. In Greece, breaking and scattering of pomegranate seeds was the favourite symbol. In the Song of Solomon (Bible, v.1) in wedding feast there is a reference to the juice of pomegranate seeds.

As already mentioned, figures and images of fish figure prominently in the wedding ceremonies of many communities in India as a symbol of fertility since fish is known to multiply very fast.

In Jewish weddings even to this day, immediately after the wedding, the congregation is expected to shout out, "Be fruitful and multiply". Fertility rites can also be traced to the custom of honeymoon (called 'Madhuchandrika' in Sanskrit), as discussed below.

14.4   Honeymoon

The word "honeymoon" originated with the ancient Teutons (of Germany), meaning 'away from home'. For details see Paula Scher, *The Honeymoon Book*, M.Evans and Co., New York, 1981.

According to one legend, son of Attila, the celebrated king of the Huns fell in love with a beautiful slave girl who was previously married and became a widow. She was believed to have been infertile. The king was totally against his son's marriage to this slave girl. But the prince secretly married her and ran away from home. Attila was so angry that he banished them from the kingdom.

But the king had no other son as his successor to the throne. Later, the king instead of disowning him decreed that he would recognize the marriage if his slave wife would bear a male successor to his son.

There was a belief that *Mead* , a kind of wine made mainly with honey, and fermented with egg yolk, corn syrup and spices including juice of pomegranate seeds taken on a full moon night enhanced sexual appetite and increased fertility. The newly wed couple drank this wine while in exile and had in course of time several male issues. It is hard to confirm whether this is indeed the origin of what we know of honeymoon today as the custom of going away after wedding from the bridegroom's home for a period of time. However, there is some medical evidence that suggests that egg yolk increases sexual prowess and fertility.

14.5   Warding off Evil Spirits

There is a common superstition that evil spirits hover around a marriage, and the couple is a target for them.
After church marriages, a concerto of car-horns appears to reflect the same age-old fear of evil spirits and warding them off by loud sounds. Louder the sounds the better it is. These sounds intimidate the evil spirits.
In olden days it was customary to ring bells and blow trumpets very loudly to intimidate evil spirits. It is believed that blowing conch-shells and trumpets in Hindu wedding ceremonies has the same purpose. Women of Bengal utter a peculiar sound like 'ulu ulu'.
A reference to the sound of 'ulu ulu' exists in the Atharva-Veda (III. 19.6) where it is used in connection with the homecoming of the king with warriors after their victory. It probably signifies a cry of joy at the victory over the evil spirits. Some eye witnesses of wedding ceremonies in Jordan and some other Arabian countries talked about the existence of such a custom there.

14.6   Rice Throwing

The custom of throwing rice in wedding ceremonies is common in many countries. A variation of this custom is to be found among Europeans throwing confetti instead of rice at the bride.
In the Eastern tradition, rice is associated with prosperity and fecundity. In a Hindu marriage, for instance, the bride's father gives

the bridegroom rice which he sprinkles on the bride three times praying for her prosperity and fecundity. The bridegroom in turn does the same to the bride. A variation of this is found in the province of Assam where rice is put in a betel-leaf with a betel nut and these are exchanged praying for one another's prosperity and fecundity.

According to some social historians, the custom is believed to have been practiced at least from the times of the Roman kingdom and gradually spread to Greece and later to other parts of Europe. Rice and other grains were the main product in a society largely dependent upon agriculture. Rice was a symbol of fertility of the earth. Throwing of rice which later on took the form of confetti became a way of wishing the bride to become fertile and help in the preservation of the race.

14.7   Knot Tying

Tying the knot is symbolic of the bond by love, affection, friendship, and respect. This custom is prevalent in different forms in almost all marriage ceremonies.

In some Hindu marriages, the ends of the clothes of the two are tied together to symbolize the bond of marital love between the two. In some other Hindu marriages, the fingers of the two are bound together with grass. It symbolizes the wish " from now onwards, our destinies are joined together ; we would enjoy prosperity together and also share poverty the same way", grass representing a natural produce signifying wealth.

According to some social historians, tying the knot at wedding is an age-old Danish custom which has survived until today among the Europeans. In a Portugese marriage ceremony, for instance, the hands of the bride and bridegroom are tied together by the church minister's stole before the ring is put on the bride's finger.

14.8   The Best Man

This appears to be a relic of the primitive age. In those days, when a man captured a wife by force, he had to depend upon the assistance of his most trusted man to help him in the seizure of the bride. This person designated as the "best man" was charged with the duty that no one interfered with the capture of the bride.

This fear of attack also possibly explains why the wife always stands on the left side of the groom---the right hand of the groom is free to take out the sword for protection, if need be.

In Christian weddings, an adult is normally chosen as the best man, usually a close and trusted friend of the bridegroom. Some believe that the function of the best man changed over time. To be the best man is an unwritten form of a commitment that he will protect the bride in the bridegroom's absence.

A variation of this custom of having the best man is found in a different form in Indian marriages. Instead of an adult, a small boy usually accompanies the bridegroom and remains close to him during the wedding ceremony.

Chapter 15

Arranged Marriage And Courtship

- Introduction

A traditional arranged marriage means that negotiations relating to a marriage are initiated and finalised by parents (or some senior family members of the two sides in the absence of their parents). The bride and groom play a relatively minor role, if at all. It would be impossible to say how and when this practice originated --- probably from the very beginning of human civilisation when the institution of marriage came to be established as a way of enforcing some discipline on the relation between man and woman.

Instead of footnotes, some details are placed at the end of the book under the title " Miscellaneous Notes" (MN---numbered).

Not a New Phenomenon

Contrary to popular belief, the system of arranged marriage is not unique to oriental culture, nor is it a new phenomenon in history. Also, arranged marriage is a custom and not a part of religious practice. Neither Hinduism nor Islam or Buddhism prescribes arranged marriage as a good religious practice. It evolved as a desirable social custom and has remained so until now.
Until very recently in the rural areas in the Western societies marriage negotiations were finalised, if not initiated, by parents.
Also, until very recently marriages in the royal families in many countries resulted from matrimonial alliances and the marriages of princes and princesses of two royal households have been arranged by the kings and queens. These conform to the definition of a conventional arranged marriage.

Even now exogamous marriages, that is, marriages outside one's community such as the race or religion do arouse eye brows. In many instances marriages are in varying degrees subject to approval of parents or community leaders. However, it would be fair to say that the traditional practice of arranged marriage (with little or no say by the boy or the girl) has continued to survive in the East as a more common custom than in the Western world. It is commonly found in the Indian sub-continent, a large part of the Middle East, Japan and China, among others.

- ## Arranged Marriage the Ancient Norm

In olden days, arranged marriage was the norm and marriage by free mixing of men and women and marriage by courtship was frowned upon. It was considered to be the solemn duty of the head of the household, usually the father, to arrange a suitable match for the boy or the girl when they reached the age of puberty. For girls, the age of puberty was 12 or 13 and for boys it was 16 or 17. This was the norm among the Hebrews. Any deviation from arranged marriage was unacceptable. For instance, the film *Fiddler on the Roof* shows how strongly the Jews were, and still are, attached to the custom of arranged marriage even until modern times. Similar was the custom among the Christians .

A particularly important factor that was responsible for arranged marriages was the early ages at which marriages occurred. Being young, boys and girls were not mature enough to realize the duties and responsibilities toward one another and of raising a family. The father or a fatherly figure was expected to make the decision.

- ## Arranged Marriage and Hindu Society

The practice or the custom of arranged marriage has been changing in all parts of the society in the East especially in the modern urban setting and among those who have been exposed to Western form of liberal ideas and culture. There has been a great deal of resistance among the younger generation to the traditional form of arranged marriage where the boy or the girl has hardly any say. Men and women belonging to the older generation are gradually beginning to accept it. Modern educated boys and girls are reluctant to marry exclusively according to the choice of their parents or elders. In modern times more often than not arranged marriages are subject to the consent of both the boy and the girl and dating in a limited way is tolerated by modern day parents in South Asian countries.

• In Rural Society

Rural societies have, however, been very slow to change in this direction. In India, for instance, in the rural areas the traditional form of arranged marriage still remains the norm. Where arranged marriages have had an element of force, even though well intentioned on the part of parents, they have resulted in unhappy matrimonial relationships.

Even at the risk of some generalisation, the traditional form of arranged marriage has continued to remain the norm in the rural societies. In the urban society, on the other hand, even though arranged marriage is still more common than the Western style courtship, the incidence of the latter type of marriages is on the increase.

• Some Pros and Cons

Some of the observations made below are the personal opinions of the present author and may be subject to many caveats. A fuller discussion of this aspect is beyond the scope of this book.

It is natural for all of us to wonder whether one form of marriage is decidedly better than the other.

Both men and women brought up in the Western society find it inconceivable that one should marry the other life partner without going out with him or her and assessing whether they would make a happy couple.

The advocates of traditional arranged marriages, on the other hand, find it unacceptable that the boy and girl are in a position to take all the factors into account that are needed for a harmonious married life. It is impossible to provide a straight answer but some facts are worth considering for putting the issue in the proper perspective.

First, the system of arranged marriage grew in a society where early marriage was very common. The boy or the girl was probably not mature enough to make informed decisions about a suitable partner. The parents did this for them. But times have changed and the average age at marriage has increased all across countries. The traditional argument in favour of arranged marriage, therefore, does not hold.

Second, in modern diluted forms of arranged marriages (where boys and girls have some say), compatibility of the couple is taken into consideration ---the family background, economic status and living standard, religious faith and customs, besides the personal attributes of the bride and the groom. It stands to reason that similar cultural and religious backgrounds of the two individuals tend to create less tension and conflicts. In that sense, arranged marriages, other things being the same, may have a higher probability of success.

Third, some overzealous proponents of arranged marriage often feel tempted to conclude from substantially higher incidence of divorce in the Western countries than in the East that arranged marriages are superior to the courtship type of marriages. A great deal of caution is needed in interpreting the divorce statistics. It is indeed a statistical fact that the incidence of family break ups and legal divorce in India and other parts of the sub-continent is very low as compared to the Western countries. This could be a very false inference for several reasons. Divorce statistics of South Asian countries and of the Western countries may not be comparable .

(a) Separations and divorces in South Asian countries and other countries may be understated;

(b) For institutional and cultural reasons, women in the traditional social structure have been known to be more tolerant and are used to accepting and continuing in an unhappy matrimonial relationship;

(c) Also, there is a great deal of social stigma attached to a separation or divorce in India and the oriental societies of China and Japan. Thus, cohabitation under the same roof does not necessarily indicate a happy and harmonious matrimonial relation ; and

(d)Not surprisingly, sociological studies have demonstrated that the spread of education among women, the rise of feminism, and their economic independence have contributed to marital instability in the Western society.

Some Concluding Remarks

Subject to some limitations mentioned above, it seems logical to say that because of tradition and culture rooted in the Eastern way of life, arranged marriages have a fairly reasonable chance of success and stability. As one writer has suggested, "…these older ways should not be despised : sociologists have suggested that arranged marriages, supervised by parents and founded upon contracts, and common-sense are as likely to turn out as happily as those relying upon the Western ideal of romantic love" (Margaret Baker, *Wedding Customs and Folklore*, p. 9).

However, when taken out of its cultural and institutional context, the present author believes, the system of arranged marriages may not be as successful and stable. There are growing numbers of second generation immigrants born of parents with origins in South Asian countries settled in Europe and North America. It is common knowledge that some immigrant families have tried a modified form of arranged marriage for their sons and daughters who have grown up in the Western world. For instance, marriages have been arranged between a son who has grown up in the Western environment and the girl who grew up in India. The reverse situations have also been found. There is some anecdotal evidence to suggest that girls (brides) who are brought up in the Indian cultural milieu are much more adaptable and tolerant and arranged marriages of that type have a greater chance of success. On the other hand, the process of adjustment is far more difficult for the couple in a reverse situation where the boy (groom) has grown up in the Eastern cultural environment and the girl in a Western cultural milieu.

Chapter 16

Dowry And Trousseau

16.1 Introduction

The dowry system is known to have been prevalent from time immemorial in one form or another. The earliest evidence of the prevalence of the dowry system is to be found in the Roman empire and was known as *dos*. Some historians believe that the dowry system evolved in the civilised world because of the gender imbalance. As civil wars and religious feuds were common in olden days, and men who went to war died in large numbers, women usually outnumbered men. It was simple economic law of supply and demand that dictated that a daughter's parents had to pay to secure a bridegroom. This was one form of marriage by purchase. A girl without a dowry was likely to remain unmarried.

Instead of footnotes, some details are placed at the end of the book under the title " Miscellaneous Notes" (MN---numbered).

16.2 Groom-dowry and Bridal-dowry

As already mentioned in Chapter 1, marriage by purchase in the original form , where the groom pays a bride-price, referred to in this book as "groom-dowry" prevails in many tribal societies in Africa, in some countries of Europe, China, Japan, India, and several Latin American countries, especially Peru.

The other form of dowry may be called " bridal-dowry", where the girl's father pays a price to the groom's family for accepting his daughter in marriage. This form of marriage by purchase became widespread especially in Asian countries and is still prevalent in China, Japan, and India.

16.3 Among Jews and Christians

There is ample evidence to suggest that the dowry system existed among the Jewish as well as among the Christians in the Biblical times.

Dowries did not always consist of money. Trousseau or the marriage chest is common in traditional European families. The trousseau consisted largely of jewellery. It also consisted of hand embroidered dresses, and linens which unmarried girls were encouraged to make from a young age.

In most Western countries, the dowry system has long disappeared, although it is possible to find some symbolic form of this. In some traditional Jewish wedding ceremonies, as mentioned before, the bride's father gives a coin to the bridegroom, symbolizing completion of a marriage contract.

16.4 Among Muslims

Under the Islamic law, when a woman is married it is an essential part of the marriage for the bridegroom to give her a dowry ('mahr'), which may be of any value agreed upon. This dowry is not like the old European dowry which was given by a father to a daughter on her marriage and
thence became the husband's property. Nor is the Muslim dowry like the African "bride-price" which is paid by the bridegroom to the father as a form of payment or compensation. The Muslim dowry is a gift from the bridegroom to the bride and it becomes her exclusive property. It remains her property even if she is later divorced. In the case of 'Khul' that is, divorce at the wife's request, she may be required to pay back all or part of the dowry.

16.5 Indian Sub-Continent

In the Indian Sub-Continent (India, Pakistan, Bangladesh) and in the Middle East, the dowry system still exists and somewhat surprisingly, is widely prevalent even among the well educated and cultured communities.

The bride's father is expected to give enough to the bridegroom's father to set up a new household for the newly wed couple. Some justification could be found in the olden days. It was customary for boys to be married an early age, 15 or 16. The new bridegroom did not have the means to start a new household. He needed some financial help and the bride's father was expected to provide this. The dowry system which originated as part of the general trend in ancient times has degenerated into an engine of tyranny. Whatever justification it had in olden times no longer holds at the present time. The boys in educated families do not ordinarily get married before they start earning and become financially self-sufficient. It often becomes the source of acrimonious family bickering if the bride does not bring the amount of dowry to the satisfaction of the groom's family. Due to the dowry system a marital bliss often becomes a marital curse. The birth of a daughter in a poor family becomes a parents' nightmare.

Interplay of Many Factors

The dowry system that we observe in many countries is the result of an interplay of many diverse and complex factors including cultural, demographic, and economic. It cannot be glossed over as symbolic of age-old tradition.

Some researchers have reported some empirical evidence to suggest a demographic imbalance as a factor contributing to the oppressive bridal dowry. For instance, one recent study based on sample surveys combined with Indian census data shows that there is a strong positive correlation between the proportion of females to males in the average marriageable age and the amount of dowry(for details see Vijayendra Rao," The Rising Price of Husbands: A Hedonistic Analysis of Dowry Increases in Rural India", Journal of Political Economy, 1993).

The Anti-Dowry Act was passed in India after Independence making the dowry system illegal and punishable by fine and even imprisonment. The law has been largely ineffective as dowry items or even money can be easily passed on as token gifts to the daughter. Without a drastic change in the attitude at many levels of the society it would be impossible to eliminate it.

Chapter 17

Wedding Folk Songs

Wedding songs are still a part of the celebration of a wedding in many traditional societies in the Asian, African, and Latin American countries. With urbanisation, however, this folk culture enshrined in wedding songs is disappearing slowly. The scope of this chapter is limited to a brief discusion of wedding songs in the undivided India.

This is not to suggest that wedding songs are not to be found as a tradition in other countries. In fact in many aboriginal communities in the European countries and in North America, as well as in Africa and in the Middle East, wedding songs are an integral part of the festivities in marriage ceremonies. This is, however, beyond the scope of the present book. For interesting collections of wedding songs, traditional and modern see Hal-Leonard Corporation, *The Big Book of Love and Wedding Songs*, Wisconsin, 1992 ; *Pop Songs for the Wedding* , edited by Milton Okun, Cherry Lane Music Co., 2000 ; and Hal-Leonard Corporation, *Wedding Songbook, Piano, Vocal, Guitar*, Wisconsin, 1987.

17.1 Mirror of Social Customs

The wedding songs that incorporate many centuries of folk tradition and wisdom are a mirror of the social customs, beliefs, faiths, and social and family life. Usually these are written by common folks and they are often without much formal education. These songs, however, when examined critically, indicate their love for fun and frolic, their simple sense of humour, and often deep insights into duties and responsibilities of married life.
In India, Pakistan and Bangladesh, especially in villages, wedding songs are very much a rich and living tradition.

Instead of footnotes, some details are placed at the end of the book under the title " Miscellaneous Notes" (MN---numbered).

Days before the actual wedding ceremony, womenfolk from the neighbourhood gather at the would-be bride's home to participate in singing. The girl's friends take a very prominent part in this. Often the friends of the family of the bride arrange such music parties. These resemble what we call bridal showers in Western countries. These bridal singing parties sometimes go on intermittently for weeks and the guests are treated with sweets and snacks.

In small Indian villages where every household knows almost every other, the guest list for wedding is very long and leaving out some families from the wedding celebration can cause some heart burning and bad blood. Many research reports by the World Bank and the Asian Development Bank have emphasized this kind of large unproductive expenditure as one of the causes of large family debts in Asian countries.

Mass Marriages

In recent years, several social service organizations and religious groups have taken initiatives in organizing mass marriages. In such mass marriages, some 50 marriage ceremonies are conducted and a community feast is arranged. The expenses are shared by the participants. Such mass marriages have become quite popular among the poor in the villages of Rajasthan, Bihar, and U.P. The wedding processions with brides and grooms arrive at the marriage hall on horsebacks, camels, and in bullock carts. Tents and temporary shelters are set up. Mass marriages are celebrated for a few days with folk songs, dances, and modest community feasts.

17.2 Songs at Many Stages

The wedding songs are sung on various occasions and at different stages of the wedding ----at the time of betrothal ceremony, before the marriage, at the time of arrival of the groom, and at the time of the newly married bride departing for her new home.

In wedding song gatherings in Indian and Pakistani marriages and in many Middle Eastern countries, the bride sits in the center of the gathering of friends and elderly women. They express joy , they tease , they bestow their blessings. And at the time of departure of the newly wed bride for her new home, they express their sorrow. Scholars such as William Archer and Verrier Elwin who have made extensive studies of Indian folk songs have pointed out that quite often there is no single authorship of these songs. Men and women gather in the evenings in poets' gathering ('Kabi Sabha'). These gatherings are sometimes divided into groups such as men and women, and one part of a village and another. One group suggests one line or thought, the other group is expected to suggest the next line and so on. There are often implicit or open contests among these groups. Folk songs are often passed on as oral traditions from one generation to another.

In the tribal communities, children are given lessons in folk songs and folk dancing even before they are introduced to alphabets.

17.3 Folk Songs and Symbolism

Scholars such as William Archer , Verrier Elwin, William Crooke, Dinesh C. Sen, and Doranne Jacobson have pointed out that these folksongs contain a great deal of symbolism.

- Fish is used as a symbol of fertility as it multiplies fast.
- In Bhojpuri songs 'champa' flowers symbolise beauty and romance, and ripe oranges are symbolic of fullness of breasts. Pomegranates have been linked to romance and fertility.
- In many Bengali folksongs, iron bangles that are offered to the new bride represent an instrument to ward off evil spirit. As Verrier Elwin said, evil spirits " are creatures of the Stone Age surviving to a later time and entertaining a great hatred for the new metal which brought their kingdom to an end" (quoted by William Archer,1985).

- Other objects that have been reported to have figured as symbolic are :
  corn and rice symbolising bounty of Nature and prosperity, green grass as symbolic of youthfulness, morning dew as symbolic of purity, and pomegranate as symbolic of fertility.

It has already been noted that in the Biblical accounts of marriage ceremonies pomegranate juice was popular as a fertility potion. While wedding song parties have been common in villages, they were not so common in cities of India and Pakistan.

In recent years, this tradition has reappeared. In many wealthy families, 'Sangeet' (Musical Soiree) is held several days before the actual wedding and well known professional singers and musicians are hired to perform and guests are invited to watch.

17.4 A Sample Of Bridal Songs

The wedding songs presented below are a small sample and have been collected from a variety of sources, published and unpublished. Collecting folk songs has been one of my personal hobbies for many years.

Some of the wedding songs of India included in this book have been collected through personal interviews and on requests by the author to several persons and scholars who have appropriate contacts. For others, the main sources include : collections by William Archer, Verrier Elwin, Doranne Jacobson, Dinesh Sen, C. Hayward, and Mohd. Kasimpuri.

By no means these wedding songs are fully representative of the various provinces of India or of Bangladesh. The choice has been largely determined by their ready availability to this author.

A sample of the wedding songs of India and Bangladesh is presented below. These songs can be divided under the following categories :

- *Haldi* Songs
- *Roka* Songs
- Teasing the New Couple
- Welcoming the Bride

- Mother-in-Law Songs
- *Kajali* Songs
- Marriage Sermons
- *Vidai* or Palki Songs

For a more detailed collection of wedding songs with original texts, see the forthcoming publication, Arun S. Roy, *The Wedding Songs of India: A Mirror of Social Customs.*

Haldi Songs

Haldi songs are sung at the ceremonial bath. The water is perfumed and mixed with turmeric ('haldi') paste and oil (see discussion of the significance of 'haldi' in an earlier chapter).

English translation of a Haldi song in Bengali is given below :

Lucky Girl
Oh lucky girl,
We put betel leaf in your mouth
We give in your hands the casket of betel leaves
And turmeric paste on your body.
Oh lucky girl, garland of marigolds in your neck.
Silver plate in your hand
Take bath in the turmeric water
The Lord of death is inhibited.
We put betel leaf in your mouth
And turmeric paste on your body.

Let your vermillion mark and conch shells
Remain for long.
Let your casket of betel leaf be always full.
Oh lucky girl,
We put betel leaf in your mouth
And turmeric paste on your body. (Bengali)

Serving betel leaf is a popular form of welcoming a guest in villages as tea or coffee is in the urban culture. In this folksong, it is probably symbolic of wealth and prosperity as the friends and elders are wishing that her casket of betel leaves be always full. Yama is the Lord of death and through this ceremony they are pleasing this deity and presumably imploring Him to give the would-be husband long life. This is also expressed in the wish that the vermillion mark and conch shell bangles (that only married women wear in some of the Eastern provinces) be with her for a long time.

Henna Song

In Kerala, there is no Haldi or ceremonial bath as is common in other communities. In stead there is Henna ceremony called 'Mailanji Pattu' in Malayalam. This seems to be a Muslim influence. Kerala has a large Muslim population. The following is a Mailanji song.

> Let mailanji last long
> Mailanji that is famous.
> Your mother and her friends
> Oh maiden, your friends
> And those who are close to you
> For all those who applied this
> This mailanji was auspicious.
> To see the girl with mailanji
> Come, come all friends. (Malaylam)

Roka / Jamaibandhani Songs

The groom's party arrives at the bride's house. Friends of the bride tease the groom and they say that they would not let him see the bride until he gives gifts or pays the girls for sweets. In Bihar these are called 'Roka' or obstruction songs. In some districts of Bangladesh, these are known as 'Jamaibandhani'.

This custom bears a close resemblance to the bridemaids seen in the Western wedding ceremonies (evidenced in numerous old English folklores). As already mentioned in an earlier chapter, as marriage by capture became more civilised, the custom of having bridemaids at the wedding became more common. The maiden companions of the bride would stand in front of the bride's house and would refuse to let the bridegroom and his company enter the house. The bridegroom would have to gain entrance by pleasing them with gifts. In Bengal these bridemaids are known as 'phulkumari' (flowergirls). The following is an example of Roka Song in the Bengali language :

> *Groom from Calcutta* (Kolikata)
> From the city of Kolikata, the groom has come.
> Come one and come all.
> He has a fashionable haircut
> He has put scented hair oil
> He has fashionable clothing, fashionable shoes.
> Look, the groom is looking around like a thief.
> May be he is looking for the bride.
> Oh good heavens !
> No seeing the bride with empty hands.
> Open your ears and listen Oh groom
> The bride is not in your luck
> The five flowergirls must get
> Money for the sweets.
> From the city of Calcutta, the groom has come.
> Come one and come all. (Bengali)

Teasing the new couple

The following Bengali folksong is being sung to tease the new groom and also indirectly the new bride by her friends :

Crown of Thieves
Listen, Oh crown of the thieves
You tell us what punishment we should give you.
If one steals jewellery, we take him to police station,
If one steals from our orchard, we beat him up.
There is no comparison with what you have stolen.
Our girl is a young adult but innocent she is,
You tricked her and stole her heart.
She has given up eating and sleeping,
Without seeing you she is dying. (Bengali)

Welcoming the bride

Example of a Bengali song welcoming the new bride by the elders in the groom's house is reproduced below :

Lakshmi
We welcome you new bride to our home
Come to our home—we light this lamp.
Come to our home as the goddess Lakshmi
Come to our home, we put oil and vermillion (on your forehead)
Live in this house for ever as goddess Lakhshmi
Like all fish that live happily in water.
We welcome you new bride to our home
Let your lap be full with many children
We sprinkle flowers and sandalwood paste on you. (Bengali)

Lakshmi is the goddess of wealth in Hindu mythology. The new bride is considered to be the Lakshmi of the house. A saying in Bengali is " Grihabodhur hashi mukh, Lakshmi haren sakal dukh". If the housewife has a smiling face, Goddess Lakshmi removes all sorrows . There is another saying in Bengali " Notun bouer chokher jaley dhaner khetey agun jaley" which means that if tears fall from the eyes of the new bride, the paddy field catches fire. Flowers and sandalwood paste are symbolic of giving a blessing.

Another Bengali folksong welcoming the new bride :
Betel Leaf
Here is betel leaf and betel nut and the
Iron bangle in the new bride's hands.
We put oil and vermillion on the new bride's forehead.
We put water with *Tulsi* and the earth from the bank of the
Ganges
Fruit from the pomegranate tree
The stick for the old age in the new bride's hands
Paddy and grass
The morning dew
The black soot for the eyes
A child's toy
We put oil and vermillion on the new bride's forehead. (Bengali)

This song is also replete with fertility symbols---pomegranate, and
children as walking sticks in old age. It also has references to
materials considered to be auspicious---paddy, green grass, and
morning dew.

Mangala Aathira

One song commonly sung in Kerala by womenfolk when the new
bride comes to the groom's home is called 'Mangala Aathira'.
Womenfolk sing as well as dance to the accompaniment of music.
Mangala Aathira relates a Purana story. The new beautiful bride's
husband unfortunately died on the wedding day. The bride, a devotee
of Parvathi prayed to her with her heart and soul. Goddess Parvathi
was moved and went to Sree Parameswara and requested him to give
back the husband's life. Unless this was done, Parvathi threatened
that she will live the ascetic life of a widow and will not have any
contact with Lord Shiva, Goddess Parvathi's husband. Being
approached by Parameswara, Yama, Lord of death restored the new
groom to life. They lived happily ever after.
It is believed that singing of this song prolongs the married life of the
newly married couple.
This is a long folksong, only the last stanza is reproduced below.

Devi Parvathi went to see Parameswara
Request she made to give back
The bridegroom's life.
If not, she will live like a widow
Hair will be uncombed and flowing
No contact with Lord Shiva.
....
Those women who sing this song
A long happy married life they will have.
Wealth and children they will have
Many relatives they will have
Children will live long
And happy marriages they will have. (Malaylam)

Mother-in-law songs

In olden days, the new brides were very young and the mother-in-law
was the dominant figure in the family. Verbal encounters with the
mother-in-law have been known to be rare in the traditional Indian
society. This folksong is an interesting one and mocks at the mother-
in-law. An English translation is provided below.

Bride's Disappointment
The mother-in-law says :
"Half the day goes by for the bride to fetch a pitcher of water
(from the river)
I wonder at the new bride's work.
Before the wedding the matchmaker said
There is none equal to her in household work
In this district.
She gasps in cooking a pot of rice.
What a calamity after bringing the new bride!"

The new bride says :
"Before marriage I had heard that

I am married in a royal house.
I will sit all day on a chair with betel leaf in my mouth.
The servants will compete with one another to take orders.
I will eat from the dish made of silver and dainty rice
Oh father, what kind of royal house have you married me into !"
(Bengali)

In remote villages in olden days, when tubewells were not so common, water from the nearby lake or river was the main water supply for the household. Housewives used to fetch this for the family in earthen pots.

Kajali songs

In poor villages without adequate employment opportunities, the husband often has to go to a more prosperous village or city for work, away from the ancestral land, leaving his wife with other family members. The bride is lonely and longs for the husband's company. In Bihar these are called 'Kajali' songs.

A Bhojpuri song is reproduced below by way of an illustration.

'Sawan' is the month of monsoon and is romantically associated with many songs, poetry and other forms of art in India.

Month of Sawan
　　Sawan and the leaping, reeling rain
　　How the heart longs, O my friend.
　　. . . . .
　　Gusts of wind
　　Scatter the drizzling rain
　　But yet my heart's thief does not come,
　　Sawan and the leaping, reeling rain. (Bhojpuri)

In the following song, the village bride who was probably married at a very early age, expresses the pain of loneliness. Her husband has been away at a distant place to earn a better livelihood for the family. She announces that now she is a beautiful grown up adult woman.

Distand Land
How the heart longs, O my friend.
You have gone to a distant land
They tell me.
You have gone to a distant land
They tell me.
You will return when you are rich.
You will return when you are rich.
My friends tease me you have found a pretty girl.
I do not believe them , my love.

A young innocent girl I am not
A full grown woman I am
My love.
My body is like a river in spate.
My arms are the creepers of
Champa plant.
My breasts are full like ripened oranges.
A young innocent girl I am not
A full grown woman I am
My love. (Bhojpuri)

In the following song, a newly wed Muslim wife speaks of her anguish as her husband has been away from the village for three monsoons and it seems to her that she has not seen her husband for a thousand years. She is shy about telling it to anybody in the house. She says that the doctor brought from the city has no clue why she has fallen sick.

Doctor from the city
What will the doctor from the city will do to me ?
Whom shall I tell the agony of my heart ?
My in-laws are thinking
I have fallen sick.

One in whose heart fire burns
The doctor has given medicine for her stomach !

Three monsoons have come and gone
It is hard to remain at home.
Allah, why did you arrange my marriage ?
It seems I have not seen him for a thousand years
What will the doctor from the city will do to me ?
Whom shall I tell the agony of my heart ? (Bengali)

Marriage sermons

The following is a song in the Malayalam language, spoken by people
of Kerala. Village women are giving sermons to the bride and asking
her to be loyal to her husband and follow the example of legendary
Sita, wife of Lord Rama (of the Ramayana mythology) .

Be Happy
Be happy our darling girl.
Bring honor to your mother and father.
Bring honor to your mother and father.
Be a housewife like Sita
Who sacrificed her comforts for Lord Rama.
Think of your husband as your only man.
The thought of another man
Is like the thought of wild fire.
The greedy touch of another man
Is like the touch of a poisonous snake.
Be happy our darling girl.
Bring honor to your mother and father. (Malaylam)

The following is also a song in the Malaylam language. The bride's girlfriends are giving the new bride sermons not to surrender to her husband too easily.

Oh beauty
Oh beauty,
Do not be a fool and do not surrender.
Do not surrender,
Do not surrender.
Surrender if you do
You will regret all your life.
Do not be a fool and do not surrender.

Do not be a fool and do not surrender.
Let him beg and let him fall on your feet.
When he falls on your feet, surrender.
Love him with your heart and soul
Make him the jewel of your life. (Malaylam)

Departure of the bride (Vidai/Palki songs)

Wedding is a very joyous occasion that brings the happiness and fulfillment in many ways. But there is also an underlying current of sadness as the married girl leaves for her new home and new family. Many folk songs give expression to this sadness as the girl's parents, brothers, and sisters say farewell to the bride. These are also known as 'Vidai' songs.

The Doli
The Doli is here.
Our maiden is going to her father-in-law's house.
She is the lucky one
She is the blessed one.
Sprinkle flowers on the Doli, Oh ladies.
The Doli is here.
Our maiden is going to her father-in-law's house. (Hindi)

This kind of a song is sung at the time of departure of the bride to her new home. *Doli* (also called Palki in some places) is the traditional Indian palanquin used to carry the newly married couple to the husband's house. It is manually carried by several bearers. It is tastefully decorated with flowers and other materials. In olden days when means of transportation were poor and the access to villages was not available through trains, buses, and other modern means, PALKI was very commonly used for carrying the newly wed couple from the bride's to the groom's house. Even these days Palki is used in remote villages. There seems to have been a revival of 'doli' to carry the new bride for some distance in cities to recapture the past tradition.

We Got a Prince

A prince we got as groom
As a princess my daughter will rule.
Say good-bye to her with all happiness
The streets will be crowded
The 'doli' will be on many shoulders
She will feel some sadness in the 'doli'.

She will turn the new house into a heaven
She will bring respect to both the families.
This is the blessing her father gives.

Daughters belong to other households
Nobody has been able to keep her with them.
Don't so sad feel
Say good-bye to her with all happiness
A prince we got as groom
As a princess my daughter will rule. (Hindi)

The above song reflects the sentiments and thoughts of the bride's father while saying good-bye to her.

Lift the Palki

Lift the Palki, lift the Palki
Lift the Palki Jhum Jhuma
Go forward, go forward
Go forward Jhum Jhuma.

At front and back look carefully
The new bride is with us
Go forward, go forward
Go forward Jhum Jhuma.

The new bride is sad
She had to leave her parental home.
Go forward, go forward
Go forward Jhum Jhuma.

Colourful bangles in her hand
Make musical sounds.
Go forward, go forward
Go forward Jhum Jhuma.

Cry not new bride, we would reach soon
Your father-in-law's home.
You would be the queen of the house.
Go forward, go forward
Go forward Jhum Jhuma. (Bengali)

The Doli and the New Home
The Doli is here our darling girl.
This Doli is for you.
Go to your new home
And make it your home.

Give your heart and give your love
Make them your own.

That is where you belong, our darling girl.
The Doli is here our darling girl.
When you come, you will come with 'sindur'
And grandsons for us.
The Doli is here, our darling girl. (Bhojpuri)

After carrying and walking a couple of miles, the carriers of the Palki
would need rest. Children would come around and broadcast the
news to their mothers that a new bride is passing through the village.
The housewives of the village would come and give their blessings to
the new bride even though she is a stranger. They would serve the
groom's party with drinking water, and sweets. At this time they
would sing some songs also.

> *Whose house are you going to*
> Which village do you belong to and
> Whose house are you going to ?
> Raise the veil oh new bride and show your face.
> We put the sugar drink in your hand, chew pan and betel nut
> Let your house be filled with children
> And get love from your husband. (Bengali)

In turn it is expected that the new groom would reciprocate the
gesture by distributing sweets to the children who have gathered see
the new bride.
As mentioned, a wider variety of wedding songs, some with original
texts can be found in the forthcoming publication, Arun S. Roy, The
Wedding Songs of India : A Mirror of Social Customs and Tradition

Chapter 18

Wedding Superstitions

Superstitions in numerous forms have been a part of human civilization and we have inherited them from time immomerial. Many of these superstitions are still with us. These superstitions are observed although no reason is known or no rational justification can always be found.

> Instead of footnotes, some details are placed at the end of the book under the title " Miscellaneous Notes" (MN---numbered).

First, the superstitions arose out of fear of the evil spirit or witchcraft. The ancient man had little protection from the wrath of Nature—flood, hurricane, earthquake, pestilence, draught, and other natural disasters.

Secondly, people had been completely dependent upon Nature for survival and sustenance. For their happiness and prosperity they tried to propitiate good spirits or gods.

Thirdly, the man in tribal age found strength in numbers and tribal wars took a heavy toll. For the survival of a tribe it was essential to have a large population. For this reason fertility was considered a blessing and sterility a curse.

There are numerous superstitions relating to marriage that are still observed, while there are others which have disappeared with passage of time.

* In England and Scotland, if a bridal party meets a funeral or a black cat on its way to the church it is considered as ominous.

It must turn back some distance and start the journey to the church all over again. In fact in India seeing a black cat on the way to any new activity or business such as going for a job interview or starting a new business is considered as inauspicious. The person must turn back and start his journey all over again. In Christian marriages it is also advisable for a bridal procession to avoid a cemetery on its way.

- Sneezing by the church minister at the time of conducting the marriage vow has been considered to be a bad omen. Similarly, wedding service has been known to have been postponed if either the bride or the bridegroom sneezes at the time of taking marriage vows.

Some social historians think that the origin of this superstition can be traced to ancient times when plague was a terrible disease and often became an epidemic---sneezing was the first sign of plague. It was considered as god's disapproval of the act.

In Leviticus, the Lord warns, " Then if you contrary to me…..,I will bring more plagues upon, seven-fold as many as your sins (Leviticus, 26 : 21)

The Second Book of Samuel (24:21) describes that when the Lord became angry with Israel and sent an angel to inflict punishment with plague, David built an altar and sacrificed burnt offerings, "that the plague may be averted from the people."

In the Indian subcontinent many Hindus and Muslims still consider sneezing or hearing someone sneeze an ominous sign and wait for a couple of minutes before starting a new undertaking.

- Some "wedding day superstitions" are quite well known and are observed in the Western marriages even to this day. For instance, in some Christian communities and among the Jews the bride and bridegroom do not see one another on the wedding day until they meet at the altar. This superstition also prevails among the Hindus.

- The wedding ring must not be tried on the wedding day and neither the wedding dress before the actual wedding ceremony.

- It is considered unlucky for the bride to break anything following the wedding day---it bodes lack of harmony with her husband's relatives.

- Fertility rituals and customs have existed from the primitive ages and are still observed in various forms in almost all wedding ceremonies around the world. As already discussed, rice throwing, confetti throwing to the bride and bridegroom in Christian marriages is supposed to propitiate the goddess of fertility.

- Number 13 is considered to be an unlucky number in many Western countries. In USA and Canada, in a multi-storied building naming a floor as 13 is often avoided. Due to the same superstition 13th day of the month is usually avoided for wedding. Birthday of the bride and a full moon day are considered to be very auspicious days for wedding.

- In the province of West Bengal in India, if a butterfly enters a house in a full moon night, it is believed to be a sure sign that soon there will be marriage in the house. If the butterfly sits on the body of a particular person he or she is likely to get married. According to Hindu mythology *Kama* is the god of love (of Kamasutra fame) riding on a parrot and surrounded by butterflies (*prajapati*). All Hindu wedding ceremonies begin with a saluation to Kamadeva and prajapati. Butterflies have a special symbolic significance in that they carry pollen from flower to flower thereby giving the power of fertility.

Chapter 19

Collected Proverbs and Jokes on Marriage

- Marriage is a three ring circus: engagement ring, wedding ring, and suffe-ring.
- By all means marry. If you get a good wife, you'll be happy. If you get a bad one, you'll become a philosopher...and that is a good thing for any man. - Socrates
- A successful man is one who makes more money than his wife can spend. A successful woman is one who can find such a man. - Lana Turner
- Marriage is not a word; it is a sentence.
- Marriage is when a man and woman become as one; the trouble starts when they try to decide which one.
- Marriages are made in heaven. But so again, are thunder and lightning.
- Before marriage, a man yearns for the woman he loves. After marriage, the 'Y' becomes silent and he earns for the woman he loves.
- Take a vine of a good soil, and a daughter of a good mother.—Italian Proverb
- God did not make woman from man's head, that he should rule over her ; nor from his feet, that she should be his slave ; but from his side, that she should be near his heart.---Talmud Proverb
- Marry in September's shine,
  Your living will be rich and fine.
  If in October you do marry
  Love will come but riches tarry.
  If you wed in black November,
  Only joy will come remember.
  When December's showers fall fast,
  Marry and true love will last. --English folklore

- If wed on birthday of the bride, the marriage is sure to bring joy and pride. - English folklore
- The most precious thing in life that money cannot buy is love - Anonymous
- Houses and wealth are inherited from parents but a prudent wife is from the Lord. - Bible.
- With money you can buy justice, you can buy obedience, you can buy comfort, but nobody can buy true love.
- A married man can get by with two hands but a married woman should pray for two more.
- Wives are young men's mistresses, companions for middle age, and old men's nurses. - Francis Bacon
- But I had not quite fixed whether to make him (Don Juan) end in hell —or in an unhappy marriage - not knowing which would be more severe.
  - Byron
- Marriage is not a simple love affair, it's an ordeal, and the ordeal is the sacrifice of ego to a relationship in which two have become one.
  - Joseph Cambell
- When people get married because they think it's a long-time love affair, they will be divorced very soon, because all love affairs end in disappointment. But marriage is a recognition of a spiritual identity.
  - Joseph Cambell
- For the first five years of married life, husband talks and wife listens, for the next five years the wife talks and husband listens, for rest of the years both husband and wife talk and the neighbours listen.

APPENDIX A

TABLE 1

MAJOR LIVING RELIGIONS OF THE WORLD , BY CHRONOLOGY AND POPULATION

Religion/ Approx. Age	Land Of origin	Name of Founder	Approx. Era	Follower Pop.	Percent of world pop.
Hinduism** 5,000 to 6000 years	India	No single founder	[3000-4000 B.C]	900 million	15
Judaism* 4000 years	Arabia	Abraham	[2500B.C.]	15 million	0.25
Zoroastrianism* 3,000 years	Iran	Zarathrustra	[1000B.C.]		---
Buddhism* 2,600 years	India	Gautama Buddha	[6th century B.C.]	320 million	0.06
Jainism* 2,600 years	India	Mahavira	[6th century B.C.]	4 million	---
Christianity* 2,000 years	Arabia	Jesus Christ	2,000 years [C.E.]	2000 million	33
Islam* 1,400 years	Arabia	Hazrat Muhammad	[6th century C.E.]	1200 million	20
Sikhism* 500 years	India	Guru Nanak	[15th century C.E.]	20 million	0.3

Notes : These are rounded and approximate numbers.
Sources :
*Lewis M. Hopfe and Mark R. Woodward, *Religions of the World*. Also see World Jewish Congress, *The Jewish Population of the World*, Lerner Publication Company, 1998.
** Determining the age of Hinduism has been substantially more speculative than in the case of other religions. Based on the more recent research in Indian history, Hinduism is now believed to be older than originally thought. See MN-1 in Miscellaneous Notes and

for more details on this debate, see Georg Feuerstein, Subhash Kak, and David Frawley, *In Search of the Cradle of Civilization : New Light on Ancient India*, Quest Books, Wheaton, IL : 1995.

TABLE 2

DISTRIBUTION OF POPULATION OF INDIA, BY RELIGIOUS GROUP

Religion	Percentage (rounded)
1. Hindus (688 million)	82
2. Muslims (101 million)	12
3. Christians (19.6 million)	2
4. Sikhs (16.2 million)	2
5. Buddhists (6.4 million)	Less than 1
6. Jains (3.4 million)	Less than 1
All others/Not stated	Less than 1

Source : Census of India, 1991. Total population was 838.5 million. Census of India, 2001 was not available showing distribution by religion at the time of publication of this book. There are approximately 100,000 people who are followers of the Jewish faith.

TABLE 3

DISTRIBUTION OF POPULATION OF INDIA, BY LANGUAGE

Language spoken	Percentage (rounded)
1. Hindi (337 million)	40
2. Bengali (70 million)	8
3. Telegu (66 million)	8
4. Marathi (62 million)	7
5. Tamil (53 million)	6
6. Urdu (43 million)	5
7. Gujarati (41 million)	5

8. Kannada (33 million)	4
9. Malayalam (30 million)	4
10. Oriya (28 million)	3
11. Punjabi (23 million)	3
12. Assamese (13 million)	2
13. Sindhi (2.1 million)	Less than 1
All others	5

Source : Census of India, 1991. Total population was 838.5 million.
Census of India, 2001 was not available showing distribution by
language at the time of publication of this book.

Marital Vows Taken by Queen Elizabeth II of England and Prince Philip : An Example of the Protestant Wedding Ceremony

SOLEMNIZATION OF MATRIMONY

At the day and time appointed for solemnization of Matrimony, the persons to be married shall come into the body of the Church with their friends and neighbours : and there standing together, the Man on the right hand and the Woman on the left, THE DEAN shall say

DEARLY beloved, we are gathered together here in the sight of God, and in the face of this congregation, to join together this Man and this Woman in holy Matrimony ; which is an honourable estate, instituted of God himself, signifying unto us the mystical union that is betwixt Christ and his Church ; which holy estate Christ adorned and beautified with his presence, and first miracle that he wrought, in Cana of Galilee ; and is commended in Holy Writ to be honourable among all men ; and therefore is not by any to be enterprised, nor taken in hand, unadvisedly, lightly, or wantonly ; but reverently, discreetly, soberly, and in the fear of God, duly considering the causes for which Matrimony was ordained.

First, It was ordained for the increase of mankind according to the will of God and that children might be brought up in the fear and nurture of the Lord, and to the praise of his holy Name.

Secondly, It was ordained in order that the natural affections implanted by God should be hallowed and controlled ; that those who are called of God to this holy estate should live chastely in matrimony, and thus in holiness and pureness of living mankind should dwell together in families.

Thirdly, It was ordained for the mutual society, help, and comfort, that the one ought to have of the other, both in prosperity and adversity.

Into which holy estate these two persons present come now to be joined. Therefore if any man can shew any just cause, why they may not lawfully be joined together let him now speak, or else hereafter for ever hold his peace.

Then speaking unto the persons that shall be married, THE ARCHBISHOP OF CANTERBURY shall say

I REQUIRE and charge you both, as ye will answer at the dreadful day of judgment when the secrets of all hearts shall be disclosed, that if either of you know any impediment, why ye may not be lawfully joined together in Matrimony, ye do now confess it. For be ye well assured, that so many as are coupled together otherwise than God's word doth allow are not joined together by God ; neither is their Matrimony lawful.

If no impediment be alleged, then shall the Archbishop say unto the Man PHILIP, wilt thou have this Woman to thy wedded wife, to live together after God's ordinance in the holy estate of Matrimony ? Wilt thou love her, comfort her, honour, and keep her in sickness and in health ; and, forsaking all other, keep thee only unto her, so long as ye both shall live ?

The Man shall answer
I will.

Then shall the Archbishop say unto the Woman

ELIZABETH ALEXANDRA MARY, wilt thou have this Man to thy wedded husband, to live together after God's ordinance in the holy estate of Matrimony ? Wilt thou obey him, and serve him, love, honour, and keep him in sickness and in health ; and, forsaking all other, keep thee only unto him, so long as ye both shall live ?

The Woman shall answer
I will.

Then shall the Archbishop say

Who giveth this Woman to be married to this Man ?

Then shall they give their troth to each other in this manner
The Archbishop, receiving the Woman at her father's hands, shall cause the
Man with his right hand to take the Woman by her right hand, and to
say after him as followeth

I PHILIP take thee ELIZABETH ALEXANDRA MARY
to my wedded wife, to have and to hold from this day
forward, for better for worse, for richer for poorer, in sickness
and in health, to love and to cherish, till death us do part,
according to God's holy ordinance ; and thereto I plight thee
my troth.

Then shall they loose their hands ; and the Woman with her right hand
taking the Man by his right hand, shall likewise say after the Archbishop

I ELIZABETH ALEXANDRA MARY take thee PHILIP
to my wedded husband, to have and to hold from this
day forward, for better for worse, for richer for poorer, in
sickness and in health, to love, cherish, and to obey, till death
us do part, according to God's holy ordinance ; and thereto
I give thee my troth.

Then shall they again loose their hands ; and the Man shall give unto the
Woman a Ring, laying the same upon the book. And the Archbishop,
taking the Ring, shall deliver it unto the Man to put it upon the fourth
finger of the Woman's left hand. And the Man holding the Ring there,
and taught by the Archbishop, shalt say

WITH this Ring I thee wed, with my body I thee worship,
and with all my worldly goods I thee endow : In the
Name of the Father, and of the Son, and of the Holy Ghost.
Amen.

Then the Man leaving the Ring upon the fourth finger of the Woman's left hand, they shall both kneel down; THE CONGREGATION SHALL REMAIN STANDING, and the Archbishop shall say

Let us pray.

O ETERNAL God, Creator and Preserver of all mankind, Giver of all spiritual grace, the Author of everlasting life; Send thy blessing upon these thy servants, this man and this woman, whom we bless in thy Name; that these persons may surely perform and keep the vow and covenant betwixt them made (whereof this Ring given and received is a token and pledge), and may ever remain in perfect love and peace together, and live according to thy laws; through Jesus Christ our Lord. *Amen.*

Then shall the Archbishop join their right hands together, and say

Those whom God hath joined together let no man put asunder.

Then shall the Archbishop speak unto the people

FORASMUCH as PHILIP and ELIZABETH ALEXANDRA MARY have consented together in holy wedlock, and have witnessed the same before God and this company, and thereto have given and pledged their troth either to other, and have declared the same by giving and receiving of a Ring, and by joining of hands; I pronounce that they be Man and Wife together, In the Name of the Father, and of the Son, and of the Holy Ghost. Amen.

And the Archbishop shall add this Blessing

GOD the Father, God the Son, God the Holy Ghost, bless, preserve, and keep you; the Lord mercifully with his favour look upon you; and so fill you with all spiritual benediction and grace, that ye may so live together in this life, that in the world to come ye may have life everlasting. *Amen.*

Acts Relating to Marriage in India

India is a multi-racial country with residents following a variety of different religious faiths. Rights and privileges have therefore been defined for different religious groups although there are many common elements.

The following are the *major Acts* that govern the rules relating to marriage and divorce of the different religious communities in India. For more details see : *India 1998*, Ministry of Information and Broadcasting, Government of India, 1998 .

1. Indian Christian Marriage Act (1872)
2. Kazis Act (1880)
3. Anand Karaj Act (1909)
4. Child Marriage Restraint Act (1929)
5. Parsi Marriage and Divorce Act (1936)
6. Arya Marriage Validation Act XIX of 1937
7. Dissolution of Muslim Marriage Act (1939)
8. Special Marriage Act (1954)
9. Hindu Marriage Act (1955)

- The Special Marriage Act of 1954 applies to the whole of India with some minor exceptions. The Act would apply to all persons who specifically register marriages under this Act even though they are of different religious faiths.
- The Hindu Marriage Act of 1955 applies to all Hindus, and also to Buddhists. But it does not apply to Scheduled Tribes.
- The Anand Karaj Act of 1909 applies to the Sikh community.
- The Parsi Marriage and Divorce Act of 1939 governs matrimonial relations of the Parsis.
- As regards the Muslims, marriages are governed by the Muslim Personal Law (*Shariat*) enshrined in the Kazis Act of 1880 and the Dissolution of Muslim Marriage Act of 1939.
- The Child Marriage Restraint Act of 1929 now provides for age of marriage to be 21 and 18 for male and female respectively.

A MARRIAGE PRAYER

Oh Lord of the universe,
Thou art great
And endless is thy kindness.
Thou have chosen the two
To be united in matrimony.

Let their hearts be filled with
Love for thee
And love for one another.
Let their hearts be filled with
Love for truth and justice.

Make them equal partners
In sickness as in health.
Make them equal partners
In poverty as in prosperity.
Make them equal partners
In sorrow as in happiness.
Make them at peace with one another,
Make them at peace with the world.

Give them the humility
To accept what they cannot change.
Give them the strength to
Change what they can
For their own good
And for the good of humanity.

Make their life blossom
Like a flower in the sunshine
Of thy grace.
Fill their life with the nectar of
Love and happiness.

Written by Arun S. Roy in the light of a Sufi composition.

KETUBAH
A JEWISH MARRIAGE CONTRACT

An important event in Jewish wedding is the signing and witnessing
of the Ketubah (also known as Khetuvah), marriage contract.
This contract is ordained by Mishnaic law (circa 170 CE) and
according to some authorities dates back to Biblical times. In olden
days the *ketubah,* written in Aramaic, detailed the husband's
obligations to his wife: food, clothing, dwelling and pleasure.
It also created a lien on all his property to pay her a sum of money
and support should he divorce her, or predecease her.
The document is signed by the groom and witnessed by two people,
and has the standing of a legally binding agreement, that in many
countries is enforceable by secular law.
The *ketubah* is often written as a decorative manuscript, and becomes
a work of art in itself. Many couples frame it and display it in the
house permanently.

A modern day Ketubah is reproduced below as a sample.

A Rabbi displaying the decorative Ketubah.

Text of a Sample Ketubah

The bride, ____, daughter of ____, said to the groom: "I consecrate you to me as my husband according to the laws of Moses and the traditions of our people. I shall treasure you, nourish you, and respect you as the daughters of Israel have devoted themselves to their husbands with love and integrity throughout the generations." And ____ and ____ pledged together: "We promise to be ever accepting of one another while treasuring each other's individuality; to comfort and support each other through life's disappointments and sorrows; to revel and share in each other's joys and accomplishments; to share our hopes and dreams; to strive for an intimacy that will allow us to accomplish this promise and permit us to become the persons we are yet to be. We vow to establish a home open to all of life's potential; a home filled with respect for all people; a home based on love, understanding, and the traditions of our heritage. May we live each day as the first, the last, the only day we will have with each other. All of this we take upon ourselves as valid and binding."

*Bride _____ Groom _____
*Witness _____ Witness _____
*Rabbi _____

APPENDIX B

1. A Japanese bride in a colourful traditional Kimono.

2. A bride from Punjab, a northern province of India, the majority of the population of which consists of Sikhs.

3. In a Punjabi wedding, bangles are given by the groom and the new bride must wear these as a commitment to her husband. It also signifies husband's promise to look after her during the married life.

4. Sindur-Daan in a Bengali Hindu wedding ceremony.
   The groom puts 'sindur' (red vermillion) at the parting of the hair of the new bride. It signifies her married status. Hindu widows do not wear red vermillion mark, to be distinguished from 'bindi', which is a fashion statement.

5. A galaxy of Indian brides and bridegrooms in colorful and varied outfits from different provinces of India in a demonstration of the wedding costumes of India. (Courtesy : Canadian Museum of Civilization, Ottawa)

6. A Konkani (South India) couple after their wedding ceremony. In many regions in South India, as this picture shows, fresh flowers are used as ornaments in stead of the gold and silver jewellery. (Special courtesy : Vikas Kamat)

7. In olden days, before automobiles became more popular, an Indian bridegroom came to the bride's house in a procession on horseback. This was particularly common in Rajasthan, Punjab, and U.P. In this picture, a resident of Ontario comes to the bride's house on horseback, recapturing the past tradition.

8. A traditional Buddhist wedding procession in the island of Bali, Indonesia. Bridesmaids hold ceremonial umbrellas to provide protection to the couple from evil spirits.

9. A close relative offering 'Saki' to the bride in a Japanese wedding ceremony.

10. In Moroccan Muslim weddings, called , *Fes* , there is no public signing of
a wedding contract or reciting of vows. The marriage contract is signed in
the presence of a few family members, couple of weeks before the actual
celebration, and they are considered as married upon signing such a
contract. At the wedding reception, the bride is being carried on a big
silver chair called an 'ameria'. The groom walks in front.

11. Purification ceremony in a
Japanese wedding.

12. Pala Ceremony in a Sikh Wedding. The couple circles the the Guru Granth Sahib, the sacred book of the Sikh religion. They share a shawl symbolizing that their body and soul have been spiritually united.

13. A bride from the southern province of Andhra Pradesh, India.

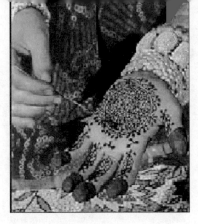

14. A bride's left palm decorated with Mehendi or Henna colour. It is believed to be the Persian influence on India when the Muslims conquered India. It has become very popular as a custom in many communities in India and abroad.

15. An Indian couple newly married according to Jain Wedding Ceremony from the Western Province of Gujarat, India. The central tenet of Jain religion is non-violence and compassion for all living beings. Their wedding ceremony very much resembles that of the Hindus except that they do not lit a fire as insects could get attracted and die.

16. Mala-Badal (exchanging flower garlands) in a Bengali Hindu Ceremony. This is comparable to exchanging rings in a Christian wedding ceremony.

17. A tribal bride from Ladakh near Kashmir, India.

18. A bride from U.P.—one of the northern provinces of India.

19. Khetubah, a decorative marriage contract in Jewish wedding.

20. 'Kanya-Daan' (also called 'Sampradaan') ceremony (bestowing the daughter by the father to the groom) in a Hindu wedding. This is an interfaith marriage.

21. Sindoor-Daan ceremony (putting vermillion mark on forehead of the bride by the groom as a symbol of married status) in a Hindu wedding.

22. Shubha-Dristi (auspicious meeting of the eyes) in a Bengali Hindu
    wedding ceremony.

23. A newly married bride
    from the hilly region of
    Himachal Pradesh,
    India.

24. A Muslim Bengali Bride
from Bangladesh

25. Laja-homa Ceremony
(offering puffed rice
to fire) in a Hindu
Wedding .

26. The "Chuppah" Ceremony in a Jewish Wedding ---symbolizing setting up
of a new home. This Chuppa is in an open space. The Chuppa resembles
the Mandap used in a Hindu Wedding Ceremony.

27. A Zoroastrian priest reciting blessings from the Zend Avesta in a Parsi
wedding ceremony.

28. A couple taking seven steps or vows (Sapta-Padi) circling fire as the witness.

29. An Indoor Chuppa in a Jewish Wedding Ceremony.

30. Phool Sajja (Bed of Flowers) or 'Suhaag Raat' (Romantic Night) after
the wedding. This is a kind of in-house honeymoon in a typical Hindu
marriage. Young girls and other relatives decorate the room in the house
and the bed with colorful flowers and trapestries. The newly wed bride
wearing a veil waits for her new husband. The husband unveils her and
spends a romantic night together. In olden days of arranged marriage,
they met like this for the first time.

31. A Christian Couple newly married in an exotic resort.

32. A newly wed
    Muslim Bride
    from Pakistan
    dressed in the
    traditional
    Pakistani wedding
    dress and
    jewellery.

33. A Pakistani Muslim groom arriving for his wedding ceremony at the
    bride's house and is being received by the host party.

34. An Indian sculpture showing a man offering a ring to her girlfriend (about 1200 years old).

35. It is an age-old tradition in many Hindu families for the new bride after coming to her husband's home to offer prayers at the Tulsi plant for health, happiness, and prosperity of the family at her new home.

36. Kadholi ceremony---collecting water for ceremonial bath ('Mangal Snan')
in a Punjabi wedding. The groom's sister-in-law along with neighbours
and friends going in a procession singing and dancing after collecting
water from a nearby river.

37. Exchanging flower garlands
(Mala-Badal) in a Hindu ceremony.

38. Palki (palanquin) used in olden days to transport a bride when the modern means of transportation were not readily available especially in rural areas, carried by two to six bearers, depending upon the size of the palanquin.

39. Palki (Palanquin) could be very artistic with intricate designs, and were used by the royal families.

40. Dolls- A Hindu Rajput couple of Rajasthan, India in traditional wedding dress.

41. 'Sindur-Daan' Ceremony, putting red vermillion on the new bride as mark of the married status in a Hindu Wedding.

42. An Arya Samaj wedding ceremony. The couple is performing the Havan or the Fire ceremony. The followers of Arya Samaj---a sect of Hinduism do not believe in idol worship and no offerings are made to any deity. Instead, offerings are made to fire as the witness of commitment to marital relationship.

43. An Indo-Canadian Bengali bride, after the wedding ceremony.

44. An Indonesian Muslim bride and a Bosnian Muslim groom. The groom is offering the Mahr which consisted of a prayer rug, the Quran and some jewellery.

45. A Japanese bride (right) with her bridesmaid.

46. "Chautha" or the fourth day after wedding in a Muslim marriage. The bride visits her parents along with the new groom after completing three days of their marriage. It is commonly believed that if both the bride and groom have fulfilled their obligations to one another as husband and wife, the angel brings a special blessing to the home of the bride. Since the bride's and groom's homes are often very far, this custom is gradually becoming out of fashion.

47. An indoor 'Mandap' (canopy) commonly used for North Indian weddings.

48. An outdoor 'Mandap' (canopy) used for many North Indian weddings.

Miscellaneous Notes

MN-1.

Sources of the Hindu Religious and Cultural Traditions

Unlike all other religions, Hinduism does not proclaim one single prophet. Instead, Hindu religious and philosophical tradition is derived from a variety of sacred texts (see below).

How old is the Hindu religion ? Since written records are scanty and archeological evidences are sketchy, this is somewhat speculative. European historians and scholars led by Max Muller believed that Hinduism dated back to the Indus Valley Civilization (1500 B.C.) and that the origins of Hinduism are to be traced to the Aryans who invaded India from Central Asia.

More recent excavations and extensive research has discarded the theory ofAryan invasion. Many historians led by Georg Feuerstein and others advocate the idea that Hinduism pre-dates the Indus Valley Civilization. It is more likely that Hinduism originated during the period 3000 B.C. to 4000 B.C. Thus there is a large consensus among historians that the Hindu religion is 5000 to 6000 years old. For more details, see Georg Feuerstein et. al.

- It is important to note that some of these scriptures were for many centuries passed on from one generation to another as oral traditions to disciples by gurus before these were written and made available to the public in general.

- In many cases, the texts of the same book (e.g., Mahabharata or Manu-Samhita) were probably written by several authors and the writing spread over many decades, as evidenced by variations in style. According to the scholars of ancient Indian history, the authorship that is generally attributed probably refers to the one who edited or compiled a particular book in its final phase.

The following table presents a list of major scriptures of the Hindu religious philosophy which have had a direct or indirect influence on the marriage customs and traditions in India, including the position of women and family structure.

	Period	Source
1. Origins of Hinduism	4,000 BC to 3000 BC	Feurestein et al (Ch.8)
2. Indus Valley Civilization	Around 1500 BC	Feurestein (p.155)
3. Vedas	1500BC to 500 BC	Hopfe (p.84)
4. Upanishads	1000 BC to 900 BC	Hopfe (p.88)
5. Ramayana	8th century BC to 7th century BC	Basham (p. 303)
6. Mahabharata	900 BC to 800 BC	Hopfe (p.96)
7. Kautilya's Arthashastra	4th century BC Reign of Chandragupta Maurya	Basham (p.164)
8. Law of Manu	300 BC to 300 AD	Hopfe (p.91)
9. Bhagavat Gita	200 BC to 200 AD	Hopfe (p.96)
10. Puranas	400 BC to 300 BC	Basham (p.299)

Sources :
George Feuerestein, Subhash Kak, and David Frawley,
In Search of the Cradle of Civilization : New Light on Ancient India, Quest
Books, Wheaton, IL : 1995.
Hopfe, L.M., *Religions of the World*, Prentice Hall, 1998.
Basham, A.L. (Ed.), *The Wonder That Was India*, Sidgwick and Jackson,
1967.

MN-2.

Kamasutra

A book on marriage customs will be considered less than
 complete without a reference to *Kamasutra*. Kamasutra, attributed to
the sage Vatsayan during the early centuries of the Christian Era has
 been regarded as a world classic on the art of making love. It goes to
such details as describing 14 types of kiss. Sexual activity was
regarded as a positive religious duty ('dharma'). Sexuality was not
looked upon as a mere vent for the animal passions of the male, but
as "a refined mutual relationship for the satisfaction of both parties."
The embracing couples depicted in the ancient Indian temples such
as Khajurah and Konarak with the ideal female figure " thick-thighed,
broad hipped, but very slender-waisted, and with heavy breasts" seem
evidently chosen for physical satisfaction of both man and woman,
comments the well known Indologist, A.L. Basham.

MN-3.

Sapta-padi or Seven Steps

For simplicity, modified translations have been provided. The couple
prays to Lord Vishnu, the Protector, and to the seven sages of
ancient India, to lead them to these seven steps.
The following are the exact texts in Sanskrit

> Step one : *Om. Ekam ise Visnus tva nayatu.*
> Step two : *Om. Dve urje Visnus tva nayatu.*
> Step three : *Om. Trini vratya Visnus tva nayatu.*
> Step four : *Om. Catvari mayo-bhavaya tva nayatu.*
> Step five : *Om. Panca pasubhyao Visnus tva nayatu.*
> Step six : *Om. Sad rayas-posaya Visnus tva nayatu.*
> Step seven : *Om. Sapta saptabhyo hotrebhyo Visnus tva nayatu .*

MN-4.

Vow of friendship

The following is the exact text in Sanskrit

> *Om. Sakha Sapta-padi bhava*

Sakhyam te gameyam.
Sakhyam te ma yosah
Sakhyam te ma yosthah.

MN-5

Comparing horoscopes

In arranged marriages, comparing the horoscopes is followed even to this day in traditional families. Also, the idea of an auspicious time for the wedding ceremony is not challenged by God-fearing Hindus. Sometimes funny situations do arise. For example, in 1974 there was a nationwide railway strike in India causing a terrible disruption in transportation. As many as 200,000 Hindu couples and their families were unable to meet on auspicious days for their marriages that were planned months and probably in some cases years in advance. A chemical engineer in Calcutta, the bridegroom, was to get married to a teacher of a high school in Bombay during this nationwide strike. The bridegroom's party hired a fleet of taxis and traveled frantically for 3 days covering a distance of 1,500 miles. When they arrived at the marriage hall, they were late by several hours. The priests went into a conference immediately and came to the conclusion that they could not get married at that late hour. After comparing the bride and bridegroom's horoscopes they decided that the earliest auspicious day was after 11 months ("Railways strike halts many Hindu weddings", *Winnipeg Free Press*, Sept. 5, 1974)

MN-6

Dissolution of marriage in Hinduism

In some books of Hindu law (e.g., Kautilya's 'Arthasatra') , marriage could be dissolved in some exceptional cases and included infertility, physical danger from his or her partner, and desertion by one of the partners exceeding a certain period of waiting.

MN-7

The original Sanskrit is :

Bhago ryama Savita Purandhar
Mayaham tva 'dur garhapatya deva.

MN-8

The Vedas (1500 BC to 500 BC)
The Vedas are the oldest Hindu scriptures and date back to at least
3500 years. 'Veda' literally means knowledge. There are four Vedas :
'Rig-veda', 'Yajur-veda', 'Sam-veda', and 'Atharva-veda'. They are
written in Sanskrit verses and contain hymns for invocations of the
gods and goddesses, prayers, rituals for various religious ceremonies,
and rules and prescriptions for household duties. See A.B. Keith, *The
Religion and Philosophy of the Veda and Upanishads*, for details.
The Vedas and Upanishads are believed to be of divine origin. These
were believed to have been heard by the ancient sages from the
Supreme Being ('Brahman'). For this reason these are also known as
'Srutis'(revealed and heard), to be distinguished from the 'Smritis'(
from memory)---the Dharmasastras, the Ramayana and Mahabharata
which were written later from memory.

MN-9
The Upanishads (1000 BC to 900 BC)
The Upanishads are about 3000 years old, and are thus slightly later
compositions than the Vedas. There are 108 Upanishads and are
written in Sanskrit verses interpersed with prose (e.g., 'Iso-
Upanishad', 'Keno-Upanishad', 'Chhandogyyo-Upanishad', to name a
few). 'Upanishad' literally means and is derived from upa-ni sad,
sitting. The implication is that these teachings were imparted by
Gurus to their pupils sitting and facing one another.
They contain the essentials of the Hindu philosophy of life and
death. They discuss the nature of existence, the soul ('Atman'), The
Supreme Being ('Brahman'), meditation, and ways of attaining
liberation ('Nirvana').

MN-10
The Bhagavat Gita (200 BC to 200 AD)
The *Bhagvat Gita* (The Celestial Song) is believed to have been
written more than 2000 years ago. It contains the essence of the
Hindu philosophy of life and death. It contains about 700 verses in
Sanskrit.

Two basic tenets of the Bhagvat Gita or Gita in short are : one, material body is transitory but the soul is immortal and indestructible ; two, we have only the duty to work but not to the fruits thereof. The Gita elaborates on 'Bhakti' and the theory of 'Karmayoga'. Also see MN-18.

MN-11

Caste and marriage

The Vedas prescribed that the bride and the groom be from the same caste. Caste still plays some role, although a less important one than in the past, in marriage fixing in the Indian society. Caste plays a more important role in matrimonial alliances in the South and in the rural areas generally.

The Vedas also prescribed that the bride and the groom should not be from the 'gotra' (clan).

One interpretation of the concept of clan is that members of a clan have the same family Guru and are likely to be descendents from the same family tree. 'Gotra's refer to the numerous names of sages (e.g., Gautam, Viswamitra, Vashist, Agastya etc.) . The possible reason for prohibition against marriage within the same 'gotra' is that it could lead to incestuous relations.

The scriptures also recommended that in the selection of the bride and bridegroom, family background and values were to be given preference over physical charm or wealth (for details see A.B. Keith, *The Religion and Philosophy of the Veda and Upanishads*, Vol. II).

MN-12

The Ramayana (8th century BC to 7th century BC)

The *Ramayana* gives descriptions of 'Swamvar' (congregation for choosing the husband) as a marriage custom in ancient India. Rama, the prince of Ayodhya (U.P.) won the hands of Sita, the princess of the kingdom of Mithila (now in Bihar) in an archery contest.

Ramayana, the older of the two epics is the story of Rama, the seventh incarnation of Lord Vishnu. It is believed to have been authored by a sage named Valmiki.

The authorship attributed to single sages (Valmiki for the Ramayana, Vyas for the Mahabharata, Vedavyas for the Bhagavat Gita, and

Manu for the Manu Samhita) needs a caveat. According to one
school of thought, the writing style of the same work differs widely
from part to part indicating that these were probably not written by
one author in one's life time. The writing was spread over a century
or so in certain cases. The single authors were more like final editors
than original composers of these mammoth works from the
beginning to the end. The Vedas and Upanishads were passed on
from one generation to the next as oral tradition for many centuries
before these were written.

The main theme consists of how Rama and his wife, Sita lived in
exile along with his brother Laxman. Rama was deprived of the
throne of Ayodhya (now in U.P.) due to a mischievous scheme by
his stepmother. While living in the forest in exile Sita was kidnapped
by Ravana, the king of the demons in Lanka (Ceylon). Rama went
into war with Ravana and finally rescued Sita. The religious
significance of the Ramayana story lies in the victory of the good
over the evil.

King Dasarath, one of the characters of the Ramayan had four
queens, indicating that in ancient India polygamy was practiced and
was acceptable.

MN-13
The Mahabharata (900 BC to 800 BC)
The *Mahabharata* , the latter of the two epics, is attributed to a sage
named Vedavyas and is believed to have been composed about 200
B.C. The Mahabharata (The Great Story of India) indicates that
polyandry was accepted and probably practiced in ancient India.
Draupadi was married to five Pandava brothers.

The proverbially voluminous story of Mahabharata (about 200,000
verses) gives a detailed account of the social and political life during
ancient times.

The central theme of the Mahabharata is the war (Battle of
Kurukshetra, between Delhi and Punjab) between the two royal
families, the Pandavas and their blood relatives, the Kauravas. The
Pandavas were deprived of their rightful kingdom by deceit by
Kauravas. Pandavas went into war with the Kauravas and was helped

in their ultimate victory by Lord Krishna, the eighth incarnation of lord Vishnu.

The dialogue between Lord Krishna and Arjun, the warrior brother of the Pandavas, on subjects of 'karma', 'yoga', religious duties, and the relation between body and soul forms the main theme of the Gita (believed to have been composed several centuries after the War of Mahabharata).

MN-14 ·
Zen and Nichiren Buddhism

Within the fold of Mahayana Buddhist sect, in China and later in USA there developed another school of Buddhism called 'Zen' ---all seekers of peace learn the real truth about Buddhism through their own experience and rational thought processes do not help. In Japan, another popular sect developed, 'Nichiren' (Sun Lotus). Its teaching was that the Lotus Sutra was the only scripture a person needed to study to become a true Buddhist.

MN-15
Manu-Samhita (300 BC to 300 AD)

Manu-Samhita or the Law of Manu laid down moral and ethical ideals for conduct. The story of Manu bears a close resemblance to the Biblical story of Noah. Manu was the only survivor along with a fish after the great deluge, according to this story.

About the authorship, some scholars are of the opinion that Manu is only a generic name and is an abbreviation for Manu-shya (mankind) and Law of Manu should be interpreted as a treatise on the Code of Ethics for Mankind.

Law of Manu exhorted that women are to be venerated for their reproductive powers. In a home "there is no difference between a woman on the one side, and wealth, beauty, and splendour, on the other". It prescribes rules for prohibiting sexual immorality, among other kinds of immorality.

The Law of Manu provided guidelines for marriage and family matters. For instance, it prescribed that an unmarried girl should be under the authority of her father, a married one under the authority of her husband, and a widow in the care of her sons.

It is the duty of a father to arrange for the marriage of his daughter before she reached the age of puberty, 12 or 13 years. Failure by the father to do so would be committing a great sin.

Some of these elements of the code of ethics can be also found in the old Jewish laws (*Talmud*). For details see L.M. Hopfe, *Religions of the World.*

The Law of Manu divided the society into four castes. These four castes are : *Brahmin* (the professional priests and scholars), *Khshatriya* (warriors), *Vaishya* (merchants), and *Shudra* (manual workers).

The caste system later became an engine of economic exploitation and social tyranny. Some scholars and interpreters are of the opinion that the caste system was not meant to be rigid and oppressive but only a convenient way to effect social division of labour.

The Law of Manu also prescribed that cows are to be respected like mothers. It prohibited the slaughtering of cows as they provide nourishment. This is in contradiction to some Vedic texts which indicate that it was a common practice in the Vedic age to offer veals as a ritual to sacrificial fires and also to eat the meat. Is it possible that sometime in history, there was a crisis such as the 'mad cow disease' as we observed in recent years ? Consequently, eating of beef was not desirable and by putting a religious stamp, the prohibition was made more acceptable. This is a speculation by the present author.

MN-16
Fasting

Muslims observe fasting during the month of Ramadan. The interpreters of Islam have emphasized several benefits of fasting : (1) it purifies body and has a spiritual significance ; (2) it gives a much needed break to the digestive system ; and (3) it makes one realise the pain of hunger and makes one more compassionate toward the hungry and starving poor. In traditional Jewish families it is customary for the bride and bridegroom to remain on fast until the wedding ceremony is over.

MN-17
Queen of the new household

The following is the text in Sanskrit:

Om. Samraggi sasure bhava.
Samraggi sasrvam bhava.
Nanandari samraggi bhava.
Samraggi adhi devrisu.

MN-18

Immortality of the Soul

When the virtuous family of Pandavas (MN- 13) was coming out victorious in the battle of Kurukshetra, Arjun of the Pandava family was devastated when he witnessed in the battlefield so many of his family members on the other side having been slaughtered . Shocked and stricken by grief, he was reluctant to fight any further even though it meant a fight for truth and justice. Lord Krishna urged Arjun not to give up and to continue the fight for truth and justice. The essence of His message was—do not be dismayed by destruction of the body, Arjun. The soul ('atman') is immortal and it never dies. One verse in the Bhagavat Gita says on the immortality of the soul,

> *Na jayate mriyate va kadachin*
> *Nayam bhutva bhabita va na bhuyah*
> *Ajo nityah sasvato yam purano*
> *Na hanyate hanyamane sarire .*

" For the soul there is neither birth nor death. Nor , having once been, does it ever cease to be. It is unborn, eternal, ever-existing, undying and primeval. It is not slain when the body is slain".

Another very popular verse from the Bhagavat Gita states on the transmigration of the soul :

> *Basangsi jirnani yatha bihaya*
> *Nabani grinhati naroparani*
> *Tatha sharirani bihaya jirnan nanyani*
> *Sanyati nabani dehi.*

Just as we change clothes when they become dirty or worn out, the soul migrates from one mortal body to another.

MN-19
Cycle of Births and Deaths
For instance, the Law of Manu stated that because of evil deeds Man is mired in the meaningless circle of births and rebirths.

> " Man obtains life of motionless (of plants etc.) as a result of the evil committed by the body, the life of birds and beasts because of the evil committed by speech, and the life of the lowest born because of the evil committed by mind." (The Law of Manu, 1:88-91).

> Man can attain liberation ('Moksha'), freedom from the cycle of birth and rebirth only through virtuous deeds.

MN-20
Widowhood
When the girl becomes a widow, as a custom she no longer wears the vermillion mark, or iron and conch shell bangles. Traditionally, she also wears only a white sari and eats only vegetarian diet. In the Southern States, among the traditional families, widows give up the 'Mangal-sutram'. In modern urban societies, however, these customs are gradually disappearing.

MN-21
Hinduism and assimilation
The inclusive, distinctively absortive and tolerant character of Hindu religion and philosophy is not to be confused with the emergence of the new Hindu fundamentalism which is largely political.

MN-22
Four Lavaans of the Sikh wedding ceremony
Description of the sacramental part of the Sikh wedding ceremony
draws heavily upon *Marriage Ceremony of the Sikhs*, Canadian Sikh
Society, Vancouver, B.C.
The Lavans (rounds) form a part of the Guru Granth Sahib. These
are reproduced below in the original text.

Lavan One

Har Phelaree lav parvirti karam driraiya bal ram jiyo
Banee brahma ved dharam driyah pap tajaia bal ram jiyo
Dharam driyah har nam dhiyavaho simrit nam driraiya
Satguru poora aaradhayo sabh kilvikh pap gavayaya
Sehaj anand hoa vadbhagee man har har meetha laaiya
Jan kahey nanak lav pehlee aarambh kaj rachaiya .

Lavan Two

Har doojaree lav satguru purakh milayia balram jiyo
Nirbhao bhey man hoyee haome mel gavaia balram jiyo
Nirmal bhao paiya hargun gaaiya har vekhe ram hadure
Har aatam ram pasariya swami sarab rahiya bharpure
Antar bahar har prabh eeke mil har jan mangal gaaye
Jan nanak dujee lav chalaee anhad sabad vajaye.

Lavan Three

Har teejaree lav man chao bhayiya beragiya bal ram jiyo
Sant jana har mel paayia vadbhagiya balram jiyo
Nirmal har paayiya har gun gaayiya mukh boli har banee
Sant jana vadhbhagee paayiya har kathiyee akath kahanee
Hirde har har har dhunee upjee har japiye mastak bhag jiyo
Jan nanak bole teejee lave har upje man berag jiyo.

Lavan Four

Har chautharee lav man sehaj bhayiya har paayiya bal ram jiyo
Gurmukh miliya subhai har man tan meetha laaiya balram jiyo
Har meetha laayiya mere prabh bhaiya andin har liv layee
Man chindia phal paaiya swami har nam vajee vadhaee
Har prabh thakur kaj rachaiya dhan hirdey nam vigaasee
Jan nanak bole chauthee lave har paayiyaa prabh avinasee.

MN-23
The other four forms of Hindu marriage are :
Daiva marriage in which a father gives his daughter to a priest as a sacrifice
Prajapatya marriage in which the father gives the girl without dowry and without demanding bride-price
Arsa marriage in which , in place of the dowry, there is a token bride-price.
Paisacha marriage in which there is seduction of a girl while asleep, mentally deranged, or drunk.

MN-24
Swamvar (Self-selection of husband)
Epic literature shows more than one form of 'swamvar' marriage was practised in ancient India. Princess Savitri toured the country in a chariot in search of a husband until she found Satyavan, a woodcutter. Damayanti chose her husband Nala from an assembly of great warriors. Rama won the hands of princess Sita at a great archery contest.

MN-25
Wife half of Man
Wife, as the sole mistress of the household, exercises control over all members of the household (Rigveda, III. 53.4). Similarly, the Adiparva of the Mahabharata gives the following honourable status to the wife in the following verse :
"The wife is half the man,
The best of friends,

The root of the three ends of life,
And of all that will help him in the other world.
Even a man in the grip of rage
Will not be harsh to a woman,
Remembering that on her depend
The joys of love, happiness, and virtue."
The ancient Indian attitude to women was in fact "ambivalent". In
the post-Vedic age especially, women were often treated as inferior in
relation to man. Many restrictions were prescribed for the freedom
and activities of a married woman and women in general. The
restrictions prescribed for widows were particularly oppressive. Many
centuries later these culminated in the cruel and shameful practice of
'Sati'. It goes to the credit of the social reformers like Raja Ram
Mohan Roy (1772-1833) and others and the British rulers to abolish
this by law and to make widow remarriage acceptable.

MN-26
Months for wedding
According to a folklore in Bengal, wedding in the month of 'Bhadra'
is considered as inauspicious as it shortens the life of the groom, as
described below :

Bhadro mashey kanyadan
Swami hobey Satyavan.
Khata khule hashen Jam
Sindur sakhar ayu kam.

Falgun mashey kanyadan
Matapitar bachey pran
Shiber moto jamai peye
Jibon katey nechey geye.

Maghmashey biyar din
Jaler bhitor shukhi meen
Ma Shoshtir kripaay tar
Putrafal anekbar.

MN-27
Hindu custom in Indian Muslim wedding
A Muslim marriage in the Indian sub-continent varies slightly from
the one that is traditionally performed in Arab countries. One can
find traces of some traditional Hindu customs having become a part
of the Muslim marriage in India. For instance, in a typical Muslim
wedding in Bengal ceremonial bath with turmeric paste and oil
figures prominently as an event. These are typical Hindu customs and
to the best of our knowledge are not to be found in Muslim wedding
elsewhere.

MN-28
Zoroastrian Benedictions
bîsyâr sâl arzânîdâr ýazashne u nyâishne
  u râdî u zôr barashne
  ashahîdâr awarê hamâ kâr
u kerfehâ tan-darôstî bât nêkî bât h'ub bât.

MN-29
Zoroastrian Prayer
ýathâ ahû vairyô
  athâ ratush ashâtcît hacâ
  vanghêush dazdâ mananghô
  shyaothananãm anghêush mazdâi
  xshathremcâ ahurâi â
  ýim drigubyô dadat vâstârem!!

MN-30
Estimates of the Jewish Population
For fear of persecution and discrimination, historically many Jews did
not report (and probably some still do not report) being Jews. For
this reason, these are considered to be "estimates". For estimates of
the distribution of Jewish population in the world, see World Jewish
Congress, *The Jewish Population of the World*, Lerner Publication
Company, 1998.

the Apostles were fishermen by trade and the foremost Apostle was Peter, widely known as "The Big Fisherman."

The Three-Step Cross
Sometimes called the Graded Cross. The three steps, from the top down, stand for Faith, Hope, and Charity. Below.

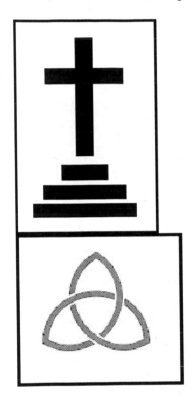

The Triquetra
The triquetra (from a Latin word meaning "three-cornered") is an ancient symbol for the Trinity. It comprises three interwoven arcs, distinct yet equal and inseparable, symbolizing that the Father, the Son, and the Holy Spirit are three distinct yet equal Persons and indivisibly One God.

Some Sacred Buddhist Symbols

MN-31
Jewish Dietary Laws
Ritual slaughter mainly refers to the method by which the animals are slaughtered for food. The Kosher method of slaughter is a quick, deep stroke across the throat with a perfectly sharp blade with no nicks or unevenness. This is recommended as the most humane method of slaughter. The Torah specifies the kinds of meat, and other food products which can and cannot be eaten by Jews. For instance, Jews are prohibited to eat pork, and camel. Also, meat must not be eaten along with dairy products, as this could interfere with the digestive process. In most cases, however, no specific reason is given for such restrictions. Many modern Jews think that the Jewish dietary laws are simply primitive health regulations that have become obsolete with modern methods of food preparation.

SOME COMMONLY USED RELIGIOUS SYMBOLS IN WEDDING AND OTHER CEREMONIES

Symbols and signs have been an integral part of the evolution of human civilization and more so as different religions came to be established. In the age of hieroglyphics, symbols and signs were the only way of communicating thoughts and expressions.

With the advent and development of alphabets, the use of symbols gradually diminished. Yet, to this day, a national flag is used to symbolize sovereignty of a nation. In almost all religions, on special occasions such as special prayers, weddings, and festivals symbols, icons, signs, and idols are used. It seems that only in Muslim culture and in Islam, use of symbols, images, and icons is non-existent or rare .

In other religions, sometimes these symbols are reminders of history or tradition of a land or culture. For instance, in Christianity fish (The Ichthus) is displayed---as a symbol used by followers of Jesus. Originally the fish was readily identifiable because most of the Apostles were fishermen by trade and the foremost Apostle was Peter, widely known as "The Big Fisherman." Tradition has it that in times of persecution, a believer would upon meeting an unknown person, use a stick to draw an arch on the ground. Then, if the newcomer was also a believer he would take the stick and draw the second arch creating the Ichthus (fish) and thus covertly identifying themselves to one another. But the same symbol does not have the same meaning or significance in all religions. The Hindus also use fish as a symbol in weddings and other special occasions. But fish in the Hindu tradition signifies fertility as the fish multiply fast. In the Buddhist tradition, on the other hand, fish is used as a symbol of fearlessness by living a life of righteousness so that one is not constantly tormented by the fear of being drowned in the vast ocean of suffering.

Lamps have been a very popular symbol of wisdom and happiness in almost all religious festivals including wedding ceremonies. In modern times the Christian churches use candlesticks. But in olden days, lamps burning with olive oil were commonly used. The Jews, Hindus, and Buddhists even to this day use decorative multi-layer lamp-stands holding a number of lamps. In the Malayl weddings in Kerala state of India, a wedding ceremony is not complete without "Deepam", a decorative multi-layer tree of lam In Jewish weddings and on other Jewish festive occasions, "Menorah", a seven-branched candelabrum is displayed. Universa and in all religions and festivities, light has come to signify the creation and beginning of life.

Similarly, flowers are used in weddings and other special occasions to celebrate the beauty and colorfulness of life. The lotu flower, for instance, has a special spiritual significance in Hindu an Buddhist religious festivities. It may also be noted in parentheses t flowers are also used in funerals and last rights as a symbol of respect, love, and affection for the departed spirit.

In some religions, idols instead of symbols and icons are u as the source of divine blessings in weddings and on other occasio In Christian churches, the idol of Jesus Christ, for instance, figures prominently as the one who blesses the couple and other participar In the Hindu wedding ceremonies and all ceremonial prayers and worship, the idol of Lord Ganesh is mandatory. Ganesh is believed to be an omnipotent god who removes all obstacles. Sometimes religious symbols represent the past history and traditio of a people. For instance, the Jewish people use Magen David, meaning "Shield of David" as the protector from evil forces and spirit.

Some Sacred Christian Symbols

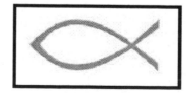

The Ichthus
The Ichthus or fish symbol is probably the oldest of all Christian symbols.Originally the fish was readily identifiable because most o

Golden Fish (Buddhist)
The golden fish symbolizes the auspiciousness of all living beings in a state of fearlessness, without danger of drowning in the ocean of sufferings, and migrating from place to place freely and spontaneously, just as fish swim freely without fear through water.

The Wheel of Dharma (Buddhist)
The golden wheel symbolizes the auspiciousness of the turning of the precious wheel of Buddha's doctrine, both in its teachings and realizations, in all realms and at all times, enabling beings to experience the joy of wholesome deeds and liberation.

Lotus Flower (Buddhist)
The lotus flower symbolizes the complete purification of the
defilements of the body, speech and mind, and the full blossoming of
wholesome deeds in blissful liberation.

Precious Umbrella (Buddhist)
The precious umbrella symbolizes the wholesome activity of
preserving beings from illness, harmful forces, and obstacles in this
life and all kinds of temporary and enduring sufferings. It also
represents the enjoyment of spiritual bliss under its cool shade.

Some Sacred Hindu Symbols

The Eternal Sound of Creation ---OM

For the Hindus & Buddhists, Om is the primordial sound, the first breath of creation, the vibration that proclaims the genesis and existence. It is made up of three Sanskrit letters, aa, au and ma which, when combined, make the sound Aum or Om. The most important symbol in Hinduism, it occurs in every prayer and invocation to most deities begins with it. Most "mantras" or hymns begin with the uttering of the sound Om.

The Katha Upanishad states, "The goal which all the Vedas declare, which all austerities aim at, and which men desire when they lead the life of continence ... is OM. This syllable OM is indeed Brahman." This symbol represents the Brahman or the Absolute -the source of all existence.

Spiritually, the sound Om signifies the pronouncement of the beginning of life or "prana" and the creation of light which destroys darkness and ignorance and heralds the beginning of all activities.

Since all life is finite and the Brahman is infinite, the sound of Om acts as a bridge between the finite and infinite. While meditating, when one chants Om, one creates within a vibration that attunes sympathy with the cosmic vibration and one starts thinking in infinite time and space.

It is interesting to observe that the significance of Om bears a close resemblance to the story of Genesis in the Bible. The syllable Om occurs even in English words having a similar meaning, for instance, 'omniscience', 'omnipotent', 'omnipresent'. Thus Om is also used to signify divinity and authority. Its similarity with the Latin 'M' as also to the Greek letter 'Omega' is discernable. Even the word 'Amen' used by Christians to conclude a prayer seems to be akin to Om.

Swastika
The Swastika (a symbol which looks like the Nazi emblem), also holds a great religious significance for the Hindus. Swastika is not a syllable or a letter, but a pictorial character in the shape of a cross with branches bent at right angles and facing in a clockwise direction. Mandatory for all religious celebrations and festivals, Swastika symbolizes the eternal nature of the Brahman, for it points in all directions, thus representing the omnipresence of the Absolute. The term 'Swastika' is believed to be a fusion of the two Sanskrit words 'Su' (good) and 'Asati' (to exist), which when combined means 'May Good Prevail'. Some Indologists say that Swastika could have represented a real structure and that in ancient times forts were built for defense reasons in a shape closely resembling the Swastika.

Menorah

One of the oldest symbols of the Jewish faith is the Menorah, a seven-branched candelabrum. The traditional Jews consider placing a Minorah with fresh wicks and olive oil as essential in a Chuppa ceremony in Jewish weddings. The illustration shown is based on instructions for construction of the menorah found in Ex. 25:31-40. Over centuries, the seven branches of the menorah came to symbolize the seven heavenly bodies and the seven days of Creation. The shape, a central shaft with three branches on either side, suggests a tree. The "tree of life" theme is common in Jewish thought , and the menorah, like the Torah, is sometimes referred to as a "tree of life."

Magen David

Magen David means "Shield" of "David". The Magen David or the hexagram [six-sided figure] was found in early remains of Jerusalem from the first century. Legend has it that God protected David from six sides - hence the origin of the Magen David, a six-pointed star. The use of David Magen is not common in modern times in weddings or other festivals. But it is believed that it was used in ancient times in Jewish weddings as a symbol of protective force.

Purnakumbha

An earthen pot or pitcher - called 'Purnakumbha' - full of water, and with fresh mango leaves and a coconut atop it, is generally placed at the door of a house where a wedding ceremony is held. Also, quite commonly it is placed by the side of the deity before starting a ceremonial worship. Purnakumbha literally means a 'full pitcher' (Sanskrit: 'purna' = full, 'kumbha' = pot). The pot symbolizes mother earth, the water life-giver, the leaves life and the coconut divine consciousness. Since the pot is always filled with water, in marriage ceremonies it signifies that with matrimony, one attains the fullness of life.

The Lotus

The lotus plant has been a symbol of spirituality in India for thousands of years among the Hindus and the Buddhists.. The life cycle of these flowers may be seen as symbolizing the evolution of the individual - who is born in darkness and strives to reach the light. The life cycle of the lotus plant begins when a Lotus seed finds its way into the sediments at the bottom of some warm little pond somewhere. Though barely able to see the light through the murky water, the new shoot strives upwards until eventually it bursts into the light, bringing the beauty of its delicate petals to the pool's surface.

The religious significance of its use in religious festivals is that the goal of all new activities and endeavors should be to strive upwards to reach the light and beauty of life.

Ganesh

Ganesh (or Ganapati) is a very popular God in India. He is called "Vighneshvara" or "Vighnaharta", the Lord of and destroyer of obstacles. People mostly worship Him asking for success in new undertakings. He is worshipped before any venture is started. He is also the God of knowledge and wisdom, and the fine arts.

One would often wonder why a revered god would have the head of an elephant. There is more than one legend in the scriptures. Perhaps the most popular story regarding Ganesha's origin is the one derived from the "Shiva Purana." Legend has it that Mother Parvati once wanted to take a bath and created a boy from her own body, asking him to stand as a guard outside while she bathed. In the meantime Lord Shiva returned home to find a stranger at his door, preventing him from entering. In anger, Shiva cut off the boy's head, upon

which Parvati was stricken with great grief. In order to cons Shiva sent out his troops (gana) to fetch the head of anyone sleeping with his head pointing to the north. Close to the ho found an elephant sleeping thus and brought back its head. S then attached the elephantine head to the body of the boy an revived him. He named the boy Ganapati or commander of H troops, and granted Him a boon that anyone would have to w Him (Ganesha) before beginning any undertaking.

Prajapati

According to Hindu mythology, Lord Brahma is the Lord of all creation, as mentioned in the Rigveda (10, 121). Prajapati literally means butterfly and butterfly is the 'vahana' or the carrier of Lord Brahma. In Hindu wedding in many parts of India, butterflies have a special symbolic significance---butterflies carry pollen from flower to flower bestowing the power of fertility. Pictures and motifs of butterflies are displayed in wedding invitation cards and in decorations of marriage halls.

Some sacred Jewish Symbols

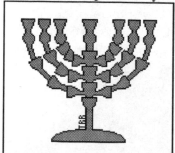

Bibliography and References

Al-Hilali, M.T. and M. H. Khan.
  The Noble Quran, In the English Language, Riyadh, 1995.
Archer, William G.,
  Songs for the Bride, Columbia University Press, 1985.
Archer, William G.,
  " An Anthology of Indian Marriage Sermons", *Man in India*, a
  journal of Indian ethnology, Vol. 23, Ranchi, 1943 .
Archer, William G.,
  "Festival Songs", *Man in India*, a journal of Indian ethnology,
  Vol. 24, Ranchi, 1944 .
Archer, W.G. and Gopal G. Soren,
  A Collection of Santal Cultivation and Marriage Songs, 1943
  (Quoted in Archer, 1985).
Baker Margaret,
  Wedding Customs and Folklore, Newton Abbot, U.K., 1977
Basham, A.L. (Ed.),
  The Wonder That Was India, Sidgwick and Jackson, Chapters 5-
  7, 1967.
Berman, Donna et al.
  When a Jew Celebrates, Berman House Inc.,N.J., 1971.
Cardozo, Arlene.
  Jewish Family Celebrations, publisher unknown, 1986
Chatterji ,S.K.,
  Arya Vedic Wedding and Initiation Ritual, Jijnasa, Calcutta, 1976
Durant, Will.
  Our Oriental Heritage, Chapters 3-4, Simon and Schuster, New
  York, 1954.
Elwin, Verrier,
  Folk Songs of Chhattisgarh, Oxford Press, 1946.
Gross, Rita M.
  Feminism and Religion, Beacon Press, 1996.
Hekmat, Anwar.
  Women and the Koran, Prometheus Books, 1997.
Henry, Edward O.

280

"North Indian Wedding Songs", *Journal of South Asian
Literature*, 1975, pp.61-93

Henry, Edward O.
Musical Culture of a North Indian Village, San Diego State
University Press, 1984.

Hopfe, L.M.
Religions of the World, Prentice Hall, 1998.

Hopkins, Thomas J.
The Hindu Religious Tradition, Encino, 1971.

Husnain, Nadeem.
Tribal India Today, Harnam Publications, New Delhi, 1983.

Ingpen, Robert and Philip Wilkinson.
A Celebration of the Customs and Rituals of the World, Oxford
University Press, 1994.

Jacobson, Doranne.
"Women's Music in Central India", *Journal of South Asian
Literature,* Vol.2, 1975.

Kamra, Ramma.
Shubh Sangeet, RSK Enterprises, Ottawa, 2001.

Kasimpuri, Mohd. Sirajuddin.
Introduction to Folksongs of Bangladesh, Bangla Academy, Dhaka,
1973.

Katz, Nathan.
Who Are the Jews of India? University of California Press,
November 2000.

Keith, A.B.
The Religion and Philosophy of the Veda and Upanishads, Vol.II,
Greenwood Press, 1971.

Lateef, Shaheeda.
Muslim Women in India, Zed Books, London, 1990.

Lester, Robert C.
Buddhhism : The Path to Nirvana, N.Y., Harper and Row, 1987.

Lipnur, Julius.
Hindus : Their Religious Beliefs and Practices, Routledge,
1994.

Majumdar, R.C.
Ancient India, Motilal Banarasidass, New Delhi, 1977.

Majumdar, R.C., H.C. Raychaudhuri, and K. Datta.
An Advanced History of India, Macmillan, London, 1967.
Mallik, Madhusudan.
Introduction to Parsee Religion, Customs, and Ceremonies.
Santiniketan: Visva-Bharati Research Publications, 1980.
Mishra, R.B.
Indian Women : Challenges and Change, Commonwealth
Publishers, New Delhi, 1992
Modi, Jivanji Jamshedji.
The Marriage Customs Among the Parsis, Bombay Press, year of
publication unknown.
O'Flaherty, Wendy.
Hindu Myths, Penguin Books, 1982.
Palsetia, Jesse S.
The Parsis of India, Brill Academic Publishers, 2001.
Pande, G.C.
Foundations of Indian Culture, Vol. II, Motilal Banarasidass,
1995.
Paul, Diana Y.
Women in Buddhism. Berkeley : University of California Press,
1985.
Rao, Vijayendra.
" The Rising Price of Husbands: A Hedonistic Analysis of
Dowry Increases in Rural India", *Journal of Political Economy*,
Aug. 1993.
Roy, Arun S.
Wedding Songs of India : Mirror of Social Customs
(forthcoming)
Roy, Arun S.
"Gender Roles", *International Encyclopedia of Social and Economic
Policy*, Routledge Publishing (forthcoming)
Roy Choudhury, P.C.
Folklore of Bihar, National Book Trust of India, New Delhi,
1976.
Saraswati, Baidyanath (Ed.).
Tribal Thought and Culture, Concept Publishing, New Delhi,
1991.

Saraswati, Baidyanath.
    Contributions to the Understanding of Indian Civilization, Karnatak
    University, Dharwar , 1970.
Sen, Dinesh C.
    The Ballads of Mymensing, 1945.
Shashi, S.S.
    Night Life of Indian Tribes, Agam Prakashan, Delhi, 1987.
Singh, Chandramani.
    Marriage Songs from the Bhojpuri Region, Kitab Mahal, Jaipur,
    1979.
Srinivas, M.N.
    Marriage and Family in Mysore, New Book Co., Bombay, 1942.
Swidler, Leonard.
    Women in Judaism, Metuchen, N.J., 1976.
Trepp, Leo.
    Judaism : Development and Life , Encino, CA, 1966.

ISBN 1412038480-0